Math Experiences for Young Learners

Developmental Activities on Numbers and Counting, Shapes, Order and Position of Objects, Patterns, and Measurement

by Marilee Woodfield

illustrated by Janet Armbrust

1 2 3 4 5

Publisher
Key Education Publishing Company, LLC
Minneapolis, Minnesota

www.keyeducationpublishing.com

CONGRATULATIONS ON YOUR PURCHASE OF A KEY EDUCATION PRODUCT!

The editors at Key Education are former teachers who bring experience, enthusiasm, and quality to each and every product. Thousands of teachers have looked to the staff at Key Education for new and innovative resources to make their work more enjoyable and rewarding. We are committed to developing educational materials that will assist teachers in building a strong and developmentally appropriate curriculum for young children.

PLAN FOR GREAT TEACHING EXPERIENCES WHEN YOU USE EDUCATIONAL MATERIALS FROM KEY EDUCATION PUBLISHING COMPANY, LLC

Credits

Author: Marilee Woodfield
Publisher: Sherrill B. Flora
Editors: Debra Olson Pressnall and Karen Seberg
Inside Illustrations: Janet Armbrust
Page Design and Layout: Key Education Staff
Cover Production: Annette Hollister-Papp
Cover Photo Credit: © Brand X and
© ShutterStock

Key Education welcomes manuscripts
and product ideas from teachers.
For a copy of our submission guidelines,
please send a self-addressed, stamped envelope to:
Key Education Publishing Company, LLC
Acquisitions Department
9601 Newton Avenue South
Minneapolis, Minnesota 55431

About the Author

Marilee Woodfield graduated with a bachelor of science in human development from Brigham Young University. In addition to teaching and directing preschools for 20 years, she has written more than 15 resource books for early childhood educators. Marilee also spends her time driving the family taxi service and completing various home-improvement projects. She currently resides in Texas with her husband and four children.

Copyright Notice

Standard Book Number: 978-1-602680-24-1
Math Experiences for Young Learners
Copyright © 2008 by Key Education Publishing Company, LLC
Minneapolis, Minnesota 55431

Table of Contents

Introduction

One of the most intrinsic concepts for young children is numbers and counting. From the time they begin to talk, children attach meaning to numbers and sets of objects. While preschoolers and kindergarten children are too young to do traditional math (and worksheets are completely inappropriate for preschoolers), there are many activities for young children that will enhance their understanding of math concepts. Giving children the opportunity to manipulate objects, practice problem-solving skills, and communicate about their experiences will foster their mathematical thinking.

It is easy to create a classroom environment where children can learn about various math concepts. You will not need any special training, just a basic understanding of what to expect (see page 6 for some general developmental guidelines). Beginning math concepts should not be viewed as challenging for young learners. Instead, offer tasks that are fun and presented in a developmentally appropriate way. Here are some strategies to consider as you incorporate math topics into your curriculum:

- Plan a variety of open-ended activities that involve individual, small group, and large group learning.

- Immerse your class in rich opportunities to investigate math concepts (see "Creating a Math Environment" on page 7).

- Recognize that there will be many different levels of understanding. It is important to guide children along a continuum of skill development by offering diverse experiences to foster mathematical thinking.

- Encourage "math talk" in your classroom for vocabulary development. Examples might include the following: "This bucket is *larger.*" "Who has the *most*?" or "What number comes after four?"

In this handy resource book, you will find:

- Ideas for creating a math environment that include suggested read-aloud picture-book titles, finger plays and action rhymes, math center ideas, little book creations, and fun activities for transition times.

- Take-home letters for activities children can do with parents to encourage math learning at home.

- Ideas for math-box games, file-folder activities, and large-group experiences that also provide opportunities for tons of hands-on learning.

Educators can use *Math Experiences for Young Learners* to help children acquire basic and appropriate mathematical knowledge:

- number concepts (counting, one-to-one correspondence, learning the meaning of numerals 1–5, 1–10, or 1–20)

- geometric shapes

- order of objects/events (*first, second, third,* or *first, middle, last*)

- relative position of objects (*above, below, beside, under, in front of,* etc.)

- matching, extending, and creating patterns

- sorting and classifying objects

- problem solving

- measuring and estimating

Each large-group lesson also provides suggestions for extending the activity, a list of materials needed, a list of skills that are used and learned while engaged in the activity, and a suggestion for integrating the featured math concept in another curriculum area.

With the information and activity suggestions offered in this book, you can be confident that you are helping children acquire a solid foundation for future math learning.

Concept Reference for Easy Planning

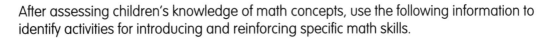

After assessing children's knowledge of math concepts, use the following information to identify activities for introducing and reinforcing specific math skills.

Numbers and Counting

Concepts and Skills: numerals, number permanence, number words, one-to-one correspondence, ordinal numbers, awareness that numbers have multiple uses, comparing quantities, counting in correct sequence, labeling collections with numerals

School-to-Home Link
Number Hunt (page 15)
Look 'n' Count (pages 16–17)

Math Box Activities
Sandpaper Numerals (page 18)
Egg Carton Sort (page 18)
Number Bracelets (page 19)
Number Wheel (page 19)
Number Cups (page 21)
Marshmallow Toss (page 21)
Counting Bugs (page 22)

File Folder Game
Catching Bugs (pages 35–38)

Large Group Activities
Shark Attack (page 45)
Take Me Out to the Ball Game (page 49)
Find Me First (page 50)
Five Is Still Five (page 54)
Snack Time Math (page 55)

Card Games
Match Up Numbers (page 57)
Go Fish for Numbers (page 57)

Geometry and Spatial Relationships

Concepts and Skills: match and name two-dimensional shapes, use shapes to make pictures, recognize geometric shapes in environment, use spatial words to place objects (directionality and position)

Math Box Activities
Shape Sort (page 19)
Shoestring Shapes (page 22)

File Folder Game
Shape Factory (pages 39–43)

Large Group Activities
Shape Stretch (pages 47 and 48)
Boxes, Boxes, Boxes (page 51)

Patterning

Concepts and Skills: copy and extend patterns, create original patterns

Math Box Activity
Candy Patterns (page 20)

File Folder Game
Bug Patterns (pages 24–26)

Large Group Activities
Sticks 'n' Stuff (page 44)

Sort and Classify

Concepts and Skills: recognize and group objects by one attribute

Math Box Activities
Egg Carton Sort (page 18)
Shape Sort (page 19)
Little and Big Things (page 20)

File Folder Games
Home Sweet Home (pages 27–31)
Big or Little? (pages 32–34)

Large Group Activities
Sticks 'n' Stuff (page 44)

Measurement

Concepts and Skills: nonstandard measurement, length, weight, comparing and ordering by size

Math Box Activities
Fill 'n' Line Up Bottles (page 20)
Simple Scale Measuring (page 21)
Junk Drawer Measuring (page 22)

Large Group Activity
How Many Steps? (pages 52 and 53)
Match My Size (page 56)

Concept Development Stages

When talking about math concepts with young children, it is important to remember that there is a wide range of abilities among children, which are influenced greatly by their experiences. For example, very young children will believe that the number of objects in a set can change if they are arranged differently, or that one elephant is more than five mice because it is larger. Knowing what you can expect when assessing prior knowledge will produce a more enjoyable time for everyone involved.

In general, children learn about numbers in an organized pattern of growth. First, they learn the names of some of the numbers. Next, they learn to count up to 10 or higher, in order. At this stage, children also begin to attach meaning to the numbers by pointing to objects (one-to-one correspondence) while counting, discovering that the last number said in the series refers to the size of a particular set of objects. At the same time, an awareness of numerals is starting to blossom. Finally, children begin to acquire a sense about numbers (numeracy) by comparing sets, using specific math vocabulary, such as *how many*, *which set is more*, and *which set is less*. This process requires being able to think logically and anticipate cause and effect. Therefore, while very young children are grasping simpler concepts such as sorting objects by color, older children are ready for estimating whether the space in their towers needs a large block or a small one. In the box below are some general guidelines for math development.

Three-Year-Olds

- Have little or no logical thinking
- Do not understand cause and effect
- Are developing small motor skills (may have difficulty picking up or putting small objects together)
- Make marks on paper but do not make recognizable numbers and shapes
- Understand simple ordinal concepts such as "first" and "last"
- Begin to recognize numerals but cannot write them
- Can recognize sets of objects up to three

Four-Year-Olds

- Begin to associate number concepts, vocabulary, and written numerals in meaningful ways
- Begin to develop an understanding of concepts of time: "yesterday," "today," or "tomorrow"
- Describe basic features of simple two-dimensional geometric shapes
- Can copy simple shapes and draw circles and squares without an example
- Can say number words and count and find groups of objects up to 10
- Understand counting and use one-to-one correspondence when counting objects
- Understand seriation such as big, bigger, biggest
- Understand that quantity does not change when sets of objects are rearranged (e.g., If you have five objects, there will always be five objects regardless of how they are positioned.)

Five-Year-Olds

- Easily count 10 or more objects; matches a set of objects with written numeral (up to 10)
- Begin to recognize patterns with numbers (e.g., When you add one to a number, it is always the next number.)
- Can make pictures with shapes
- Copy simple shape patterns
- Can make comparisons of objects based on two attributes
- Continue to build an understanding of time

Creating a Math Environment

To make counting, sorting, classifying, and patterning skills second nature for young children requires that they participate in activities that are embedded with opportunities to manipulate and explore math concepts. Consider the following suggestions for making the most of the school day.

- **Incorporate "math talk"** during class discussions and conversations with individual children. Here are some simple ways to make "math talk" a regular practice.

    - Verbalize comparisons by using the words *more than* or *less than*, *bigger* or *smaller*, *the most*, etc., at the appropriate times.

    - Talk about adding *one more* or having *one less than* . . . when counting sets of objects.

    - Use math words such as *how long, how many, how high, dividing things in half, equal parts*, and so on when children are playing in the block center, at the water/sand table, and in the dramatic play area.

    - Engage children in opportunities to use numbers to solve problems. For example, ask, "If there are three balls and four children want to play with them, can each child have a ball?" Make up story problems. "If you have three blocks and I give you one more, how many blocks would you have?"

- **Decorate the room with numbers.** Look for or display many examples of how numbers are used. Include envelopes labeled with street addresses, photographs of road signs, grocery store advertisements, menus, etc., not only in the math center but in the dramatic play area and the block corner.

Learning center activities and daily classroom events also offer wonderful opportunities for children to utilize math skills.

- **Morning Meeting**—The typical preschool or kindergarten day is broken up into smaller segments: circle time for specific curriculum areas, story time, snack time, lunchtime, outdoor playtime, and so on. Build awareness of the schedule as recognizable blocks of time. Include the calendar when discussing upcoming events to highlight the days of the week and month.

- **Literacy Center**—Books about numbers, shapes, and patterns may already sit on your bookshelves. (See "Books You Can Count On" on page 11 for additional titles.) Writing, stamping, and typing numbers in little books are all easy ways to incorporate number concepts in literacy activities. (See pages 9 and 10 for book-making ideas.)

- **Block Center**—This center is full of opportunities for experiences in comparing shapes and sizes of blocks. Building more towers that are taller than the first tower, discovering that two small blocks are the same size as one large block, or sorting the blocks by shape are all concepts children can investigate. When appropriate, have children describe the block shapes and look for those shapes in the environment.

- **Playground**—Counting your steps across the playground; climbing up, down, in, out, over, and under the play structures; playing hopscotch; counting beats while jumping rope; and taking turns on the swings are all examples of rich math experiences.

- **Snack Time**—Making sure each child has one cup, one napkin, and one snack or giving groups of children snack items that can be counted or divided into smaller equal groups are ways to practice one-to-one correspondence.

- **Science Center**—Measuring, counting, sorting, and classifying are all skills that are used in both math and science activities.

- **Math Word/Shape Wall**—Display shapes drawn on colorful card stock and photographs of featured shapes on actual objects. Write their names on word strips and include those labels on the wall, too.

Independent Math Investigations

In addition to integrating math concepts in other centers, having a math center where children can explore activities on their own terms is also a valuable instructional tool. Ideas for setting up a math center include the following:

- **Provide activities that mirror or extend concepts** that you introduce or explore with children during circle time.

- **Rotate all materials regularly** to keep children interested in math explorations.

- **Design learning opportunities** for individual and small group participation.

- **Keep the center organized** and create a system so that children have access to everything they need and can clean up the work area when they are finished.

- **Provide a table or flat surface** for children to work on.

- **Start classroom collections.** Whether it is milk jug caps, buttons, soda can tabs, or something else, it is easy to build a collection of identical or similar objects for children to count and sort. This is an economical way to gather manipulatives for your learning center.

- **Gather math-related items and other types of materials for the center.** You might consider adding some of the following items to the center for math investigations:

  - Abacus
  - Attribute blocks
  - Beads (wooden and plastic) and laces
  - Building blocks
  - Coins (play money or actual coins)
  - Dice
  - Dominoes
  - Dried beans, rice, and/or pasta shapes
  - Funnels
  - Geoboards and rubber binders
  - Geometric solids
  - Interlocking cubes
  - Magnetic shapes and numerals and a metal baking pan for the playing surface
  - Measuring cups and spoons
  - Measuring tapes
  - Meterstick and/or yardstick
  - Pattern blocks
  - Pegboards and pegs
  - Plastic containers (assorted shapes and sizes) and lids if possible
  - Poker chips
  - Sand/water table
  - Simple scales (bucket balance)
  - Stamping materials (objects and money stamps, ink pad, markers, and paper)

Making Little Books

Whether stapling a couple of pieces of together or creating a fanciful bound volume, children love making their own books. The following ideas for different kinds of little books are easy to make and children will love them. Be sure to have on hand various little books (common mini-books, shape books, paper bag books, and bound books) so that children can use them during those times when they are interested in "writing" their own math stories or recording some of their math ideas.

Paper Bag Book—This book can be large or small, depending on the size of the paper bags.

1. Open up two paper bags and cut off the bottom of each one. Also, trim off the tops to make clean edges. (See diagram A.)
2. Flatten each bag. Glue the bottom and top openings closed to make flat pages. (See diagram B.) Alternatively, the edges of the bags can be left open to create pockets that can hold an "About the Author" card, illustrations that slide out from inside the pockets, etc.
3. Stack the two bags on top of one another and then fold them in half the short way. Staple along the fold.
4. Glue 6 in. (15 cm) pieces of ribbon to the front and back flaps. (See diagram C.) Tie the ribbons together to keep the little book closed.

A (Step 1)

Cut

Cut

B (Steps 2 and 3)

Glue

Fold

Glue

C (Step 4)

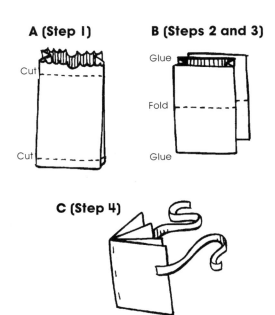

Making Little Books

Shaped Book—Any common shape can be turned into a shaped book.

1. Make one copy of the shape you wish to use.
2. Stack four or five blank pages behind the shape. Staple (or secure with a metal brad) through all layers of paper.
3. Cut through all thicknesses of paper along the outline of the shape to give the book a recognizable shape. (See illustration on right.)

Bound Book—Produce a real, bound book covered with fabric by following the steps below.

1. Cut two pieces of cardboard that are slightly larger than your book-page size.
2. Cut two pieces of quilt batting the same size as the cardboard. Glue one to each piece of cardboard.
3. Lay a piece of fabric facedown on the table. Place the two pieces of cardboard, batting side down, side by side on the fabric. Leave a small gap about 1/8 in. (3 mm) between the cardboard pieces. (See diagram A.)
4. Cut the fabric 1 in. (25 mm) longer and wider than the edges of the cardboard pieces.
5. Stretch the fabric over the cardboard edges and secure with hot glue. (See diagram B.)
6. Make a stack of several sheets of paper. Fold the stack in half to make a guide for stitching the pages to the cover (as directed in step 7). If necessary, trim so that the pages are smaller than the cardboard book cover.
7. Lay the pages on top of the cardboard cover. Carefully stitch down the middle of the papers and the cover with a sewing machine. Be sure to use craft thread and a long stitch. (See diagram C.)
8. Glue the first page of the book to the inside front cover and the last page to the inside back cover to hide the ragged edges of the fabric. Add a ribbon bookmark if desired.

A (Step 3)

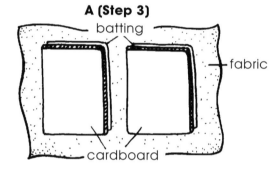

batting

fabric

cardboard

B (Step 5)

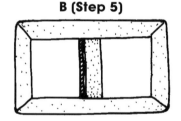

C (Step 7)

Books You Can Count On

Counting

1,2,3 to the Zoo by Eric Carle (Philomel, 1982)

Anno's Counting Book by Mitsumasa Anno (Crowell, 1977)

Caps for Sale by Esphyr Slobodkina (HarperFestival, 2008)

Cat Count by Betsy Lewin (Henry Holt, 2003)

Count! by Denise Fleming (Henry Holt, 1992)

Counting Crocodiles by Judy Sierra (Gulliver, 1997)

Dinnertime! by Sue Williams (Harcourt, 2002)

Doorbell Rang, The by Pat Hutchins (Greenwillow, 1986)

Feast for 10 by Cathryn Falwell (Clarion, 1993)

Grandma Went to Market by Stella Blackstone (Houghton Mifflin, 1996)

Hippos Go Berserk! by Sandra Boynton (Aladdin, 1996)

I Knew Two Who Said Moo by Judi Barrett (Aladdin, 2003)

Let's Count It Out, Jesse Bear by Nancy White Carlstrom (Aladdin, 2001)

Millions of Cats by Wanda Ga'g (Puffin, 2006)

Mouse Count by Ellen Stoll Walsh (Voyager, 1995)

Night Lights by Steven Schnur (Farrar, Straus and Giroux, 2000)

One Is a Snail, Ten Is a Crab: A Counting by Feet Book by April Pulley Sayre and Jeff Sayre (Candlewick, 2003)

One Moose, Twenty Mice by Clare Beaton (Barefoot Books, 2000)

One Sun Rises: An African Wildlife Counting Book by Wendy Hartmann (Dutton, 1994)

Over in the Meadow by Ezra Jack Keats (Viking Juvenile, 1999)

Quack and Count by Keith Baker (Voyager, 2004)

So Many Bunnies: A Bedtime ABC and Counting Book by Rick Walton (Lothrop, Lee & Shepard/Morrow, 1998)

Tea for Ten by Lena Anderson (R&S Books, 2000)

Ten, Nine, Eight by Molly Bang (Greenwillow, 1983)

Two Ways to Count to Ten: A Liberian Folktale by Ruby Dee (Henry Holt, 1990)

We All Went on Safari: A Counting Journey through Tanzania by Laurie Krebs (Barefoot Books, 2004)

Number Concepts

Math Counts series by Henry Pluckrose (Children's Press, 1995)

Spaghetti and Meatballs for All! A Mathematical Story by Marilyn Burns (Scholastic Press, 1997)

Twenty Is Too Many by Kate Duke (Dutton Juvenile, 2000)

What Comes in 2's, 3's, & 4's? by Suzanne Aker (Aladdin, 1992)

Patterns

Lots and Lots of Zebra Stripes: Patterns in Nature by Stephen R. Swinburne (Boyds Mills Press, 2002)

Pattern Bugs by Trudy Harris (Millbrook Press, 2001)

Pattern Fish by Trudy Harris (Millbrook Press, 2000)

Zoe's Hats: A Book of Colors and Patterns by Sharon Lane Holm (Boyds Mills Press, 2003)

Shapes

Bear in a Square by Stella Blackstone (Barefoot Books, 2006)

Greedy Triangle, The by Marilyn Burns (Scholastic Press, 1995)

Shapes, Shapes, Shapes by Tana Hoban (HarperTrophy, 1996)

When a Line Bends . . . A Shape Begins by Rhonda Gowler Greene (Houghton Mifflin, 1997)

Sizes and Measuring

Big and Little by Steve Jenkins (Houghton Mifflin, 1996)

How Big Is a Foot? by Rolf Myller (Yearling, 1991)

Is It Larger? Is It Smaller? by Tana Hoban (HarperTrophy, 1997)

Line Up Book, The by Marisabina Russo (Puffin, 1992)

Mr. Archimedes' Bath by Pamela Allen (HarperCollins, 1991)

Twelve Snails to One Lizard: A Tale of Mischief and Measurement by Susan Hightower (Simon & Schuster Children's Publishing, 1997)

Lining Up with Math Fun

While Lining Up . . .

Children can find their places by playing math games. The following are some activity suggestions:

Patterns—As children line up, have them create patterns with common attributes: the clothes they are wearing, the color of their hair, or other characteristics. Begin with simple ABAB patterns, such as "boy, girl, boy, girl." When appropriate, increase the difficulty of the task, such as creating an AAB pattern like, "sneakers, sneakers, boots." If interested, use props, such as colored cards or attribute blocks, that children can hold to build the desired pattern.

Sorting and Classifying—At first, use one attribute, such as color of shirt, tie shoes, or whether or not they are wearing socks to indicate whose turn it is to line up. When appropriate, incorporate a second characteristic to increase the difficulty, such as children who are wearing both socks and red shirts, etc.

Sequential or Ordinal—Have children line up by height—tallest to shortest or shortest to tallest. You might use ordinal numbers as children line up if you are working with a small group. For example, say, "Danny line up first. Shekira line up second." Alternatively, have children say the number that is *one more* or *one less* than the number you call out. For example, if Ryan is given the number "five," ask him to tell you the number that is one more than five as he takes his place in line.

Identifying Shapes—Create shape cards or shape necklaces and have children line up according to the shapes they are holding.

Identifying Numbers—Number cards can be used in the same way as the shape cards above. One game idea might include having children clap their hands the corresponding number of times as written on their cards. Alternatively, choose a child to be the line leader who rolls a die and asks the corresponding number of children to line up at a time.

Puzzles—During a transition time, give each child a piece of a selected jigsaw puzzle. Then, as children line up, each one places the given piece in its proper place to complete the puzzle. The activity is finished when all of the children have lined up.

"Picto-line"—Take a digital photograph of each child. Have the line leader "shuffle" the photographs like cards and then invite children to line up in the order of the photos.

While Waiting in Line . . .

Children might spend the time playing number games. Ideas include the following:

- Count up to 10 (or another number) and then back to 0.

- Count by 2s or 5s.

- Hold up a number of fingers behind your back and have children take turns guessing how many fingers are extended. If needed, offer clues to help them guess the number.

- Have children guess a "mystery" number. For example, say, "I am thinking of a number that is one more than . . ." or "I am thinking of a number that is one less than . . ." *(Mental comparison activities can be very challenging for children. Encourage them to use their fingers to figure out the mystery number.)*

- Count up and stop at a predetermined number. Have children call out the next number in order.

- Say a number (1–10) and have children hold up the corresponding number of fingers. Increase the speed as children master the skill.

- Chant a favorite finger play or action rhyme. See page 13 for some suggestions.

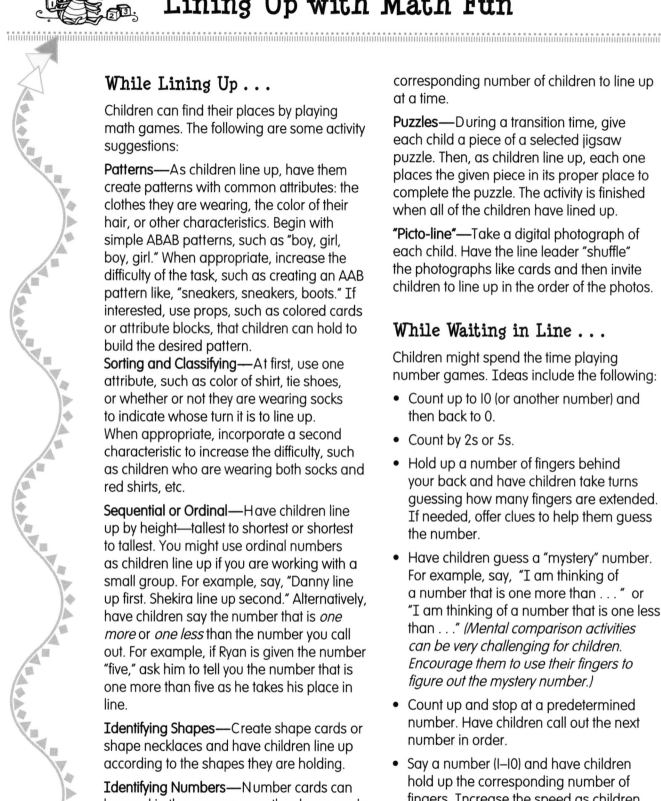

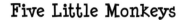

Finger Plays and Action Rhymes

Five Little Monkeys

Five little monkeys sitting in a tree,
(Use one arm for tree branch. Swing the other hand with five fingers extended below that arm.)
Teasing Mrs. Crocodile by saying,
(Place thumbs in ears and wiggle hands back and forth.)
"You can't catch me."
"You can't catch me."
Along comes Mrs. Crocodile as quiet as can be—*AND*
(Hands with palms together move slowly forward.)
SNAPPED one monkey right out of the tree!
(Clap hands on the word snapped. *)*
-*Traditional rhyme*

(Repeat the rhyme four times to count backwards to one, extending one fewer finger each time.)

Five Little Ducks

Five little ducks went out one day
Over the hills and far away.
When the mother duck said, "Quack, quack, quack,"
Four little ducks came waddling back.
(Repeat the verse three times to count from four little ducks down to one little duck. Extend fingers on one hand to show each number. Then, move body as if "waddling.")

One little duck went out one day,
Over the hills and far away.
When the mother duck said, "Quack, quack, quack,"
No little ducks came waddling back.
But when the daddy duck said, "QUACK, QUACK, QUACK!"
Five little ducks came waddling back!
-*Traditional rhyme*

1-2-3-4-5 I Caught a Fish Alive

1-2-3-4-5, I caught a fish alive.
6-7-8-9-10, I let him go again.
Why did you let him go?
Because he bit my finger so.
OH, NO!
-*Traditional rhyme*

This Old Man

This old man, he played **one**;
He played knick knack on my thumb.
With a knick knack paddy whack,
     give a dog a bone.
This old man came rolling home.

Other verses:
• This old man, he played **two**; he played knick knack on my shoe. . . .
• This old man, he played **three**; he played knick knack on my tree. . . .
• This old man, he played **four**; he played knick knack on my door. . . .
• This old man, he played **five**; he played knick knack on my hive. . . .
• This old man, he played **six**; he played knick knack on my sticks. . . .
• This old man, he played **seven**; he played knick knack up to heaven. . . .
• This old man, he played **eight**; he played knick knack on my gate. . . .
• This old man, he played **nine**; he played knick knack oh so fine. . . .
• This old man, he played **ten**; he played knick knack over again. . . .
-*Traditional rhyme and song*

Bubble Gum Chant

(Point to a different child as you say each word, stopping on the word wish.*)*

Bubble gum, bubble gum in the dish,
How many pieces do you wish?
-*Traditional rhyme*

(Selected child calls out a number. Then, everyone counts aloud up to the specified number. Repeat the chant to play again.)

Ways to Help Your Child

Dear Parent,

While rapidly growing bigger on the outside, your child is also rapidly learning new things every day, which may include number concepts! Here are some examples of math learning:

- Children learn to recite numbers by memory. At first, they may skip one or two numbers as they count, or they may reverse some numbers' order. However, soon they can rattle off the numbers from 1 to 10 (or higher) like a pro. Encourage your child to practice counting everything that is encountered during the day. For example, you might say, "Let's count the plates on the table." "Let's count how many cars we can see." Very soon, your child will learn that each number counted stands for one object in a group of objects.

- As children's mathematical thinking develops, they begin to attach meaning to numbers. They actually understand that "two" means two of something, not just the word *two*. To help your child comprehend the meaning of numbers, compare different groupings of objects that are the same in quantity. With your child, look around your home for groups of objects because you will find many. Example: Five cookies, five chairs around the table, five puppies—all stand for the number five.

- Young children can understand the concepts of "first" and "last." For example, you might say, "This looks like a great lunch. What shall we eat first?" In kindergarten, children will learn about the words *first, second,* and *third.*

So, how can you strengthen your child's number sense and counting skills? Here are some suggestions for you to consider:

- Let your child have opportunities to solve problems, such as making sure there is a place setting for each family member at the dinner table. Ask questions like "We have two cookies for four friends. What can we do?"

- Talk about numbers with your child in a playful manner. When comparing two quantities, use numbers that are only one or two more, or one or two less than the first number. For example, you might ask: "How many crayons do you have? If I gave you one more crayon, then how many would you have?" At another time, you might say: "How many crackers are on the plate? If I take one cracker off the plate, then how many will there be? Let's find out." Make good use of situations when you can take turns adding or removing an object to find out what the new quantity will be.

- Watch for math opportunities while traveling. You might look for numbers on road signs, talk about the correlation between the speed limit signs and how fast you may drive, look for flight numbers and times at the airport or train station, and so on.

- Explore the numbers involved when using recipes. Let your child help you measure the ingredients as you prepare a favorite recipe together.

Be sure to remember that learning math concepts is a step-by-step process, and formal math problems are best saved for older children. Do not demand a correct answer every time; just encourage further exploration. Most importantly, have fun with numbers.

Sincerely,

Home-to-School Link: Number Hunt

How many different ways are numbers used? To find out, conduct a number hunt with children by searching the classroom and other rooms in your school for numbers. Look for numbers on the clock, pages in a book, papers in the main office, a school bus, a street sign, the building, and so on. Then, introduce the activity below and explain to children that they will hunt for more numbers at home.

Send home a copy of the following letter and the "Hunting for Numbers!" checklist with each child. Encourage children to work with their parents to find as many numbers as possible. Plan a day when everyone can share what they learned and show their examples of numbers on things. To summarize the activity make a chart by listing all examples of numbers that the children find.

- ✂

Dear Parent,

In school, the children are learning about how numbers are used in different ways. There are numbers in and on our cars, in our homes, on our clothes, and just about anywhere we can go. Attached is a list of things on which you may find numbers. Some examples of these things with numbers can be found in your home. While you are shopping or walking in the neighborhood with your child, try to look for other examples of numbers on things and point them out to your child, too. Then, mark the related box on the checklist.

On _____ , there will be a special sharing time about numbers. *Please return the checklist on the date indicated.* For this sharing time, let your child bring an actual example, a drawing, or a digital photograph of one of the numbers that you found.

We are looking forward to seeing how many different ways numbers have been used! If you have any questions about this project, please feel free to contact me.

Sincerely,

- ✂

Name: _____   Return by: _____

Hunting for Numbers!

Look for numbers on various things. Here are some ideas for you
When your child finds a number, check the related box.

- ☐ cereal box
- ☐ clock
- ☐ clothes' sizes
- ☐ computer
- ☐ credit card
- ☐ deck of cards

- ☐ license plate
- ☐ lightbulb
- ☐ magazine
- ☐ mail envelope
- ☐ money
- ☐ newspaper

- ☐ price tag
- ☐ radio
- ☐ remote controller
- ☐ television
- ☐ thermostat
- ☐ other: _____

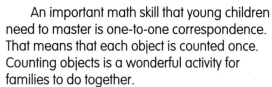

An important math skill that young children need to master is one-to-one correspondence. That means that each object is counted once. Counting objects is a wonderful activity for families to do together.

Prepare a small eight-page book for each child by stapling four sheets of paper together or by following one of the suggested ideas on pages 9 and 10. Write "My Counting Book" on the title page. Write "Other Things I Have Counted" on pages 7 and 8 of the little book.

Make a copy of the counting cards on page 17 and the parent letter below for each child. Separate the cards by cutting along the dashed lines. Place each set of cards and a little book in a zippered plastic bag. Then, staple the bag and the parent letter together.

As a class, read *The Father Who Had 10 Children* by Bénédicté Guettier (Puffin, 2001) or another favorite book on counting and talk about the many things that can be counted. Have children suggest things that can be counted at their homes. Explain the project that they will take home by showing a copy of the cards and a little book and talk about the information in the parent letter.

When children return their counting books to school, read them to the class. Make a list of the things that were counted by children. You may also wish to graph the class totals for the items. This makes it possible to show, for example, that the children counted many cars and few pillows, and so on — a powerful opportunity for comparing quantities!

Dear Parent,

I am always looking for engaging ways to encourage children to practice their counting skills. Attached are materials for a game you can play together for some counting fun.

On Monday, choose a quiet time when you and your child can be together. Have your child choose two cards randomly out of the bag. On page 2 of the little book, help your child write "On Monday, I Counted." Glue the two chosen cards below this title. Then, take time to count each featured object. If the selected topic is "doors," walk through your home and count the doors. Then, write that number in the box provided on the card. *Please be sure your child points to or touches the objects individually whenever counting. This will help reinforce the concept that the final number word said stands for the quantity of the group.* If the card suggests counting cars, you may wish to sit on your front porch or look out a window while counting the cars that pass by your home in five minutes. Continue this counting activity each day for four more days by writing the name of the day and gluing the chosen cards on each page 3–6 until all cards are used. Finally, finish pages 7 and 8 by having your child count other things of interest and write about them.

Please be sure to read the book with your child when it is completed. Then, return it to school on _____. We are looking forward to reading one another's counting stories together in class, too.

If you have any questions, please feel free to contact me. In the meantime, happy counting!

Sincerely,

trees

chairs

cars

pets

hats

pillows

apples

doors

keys

lamps

Math Box Activities

Are you looking for activity ideas that allow children the opportunity to work independently in the math center? If yes, consider making some math boxes. To do this, gather all necessary supplies for each activity and place them in designated plastic, shoe-box size or larger containers. Make a copy of the labels below and on page 23 and cut them out along the dashed lines. Laminate for durability and trim around the edges (optional). Tape the labels to the fronts of the corresponding containers. Place three or four boxes in the math center at a time and rotate the games to keep them fresh and interesting. NOTE: SOME OF THE ACTIVITIES USE SMALL OBJECTS SUCH AS DICE AND BEADS THAT MAY BE A CHOKING HAZARD.

Sandpaper Numerals

Packing the Math Box
- Sandpaper numeral cards
- Crayons
- Paper

Getting Ready: Using a stencil pattern, copy the numerals 0–9 onto coarse sandpaper by tracing around the shapes and then cut them out. Glue the sandpaper numerals onto heavy cardboard. Optional: Use other kinds of textured papers or materials to make the numeral cutouts.

How to Play: Place the paper on a numeral card. Hold a crayon lengthwise and rub it over the paper to reveal the shape of the numeral. Repeat the step with other cards.

Egg Carton Sort

Packing the Math Box
- Egg carton
- Large colorful beads
- Dried beans

Getting Ready:

For Game A, paint the bottom section of an egg carton by using a different color in each cup or in as many cups as needed, leaving some unpainted. Place several large beads that match each painted color in a zippered plastic bag for a sort-and-match task.

For Game B, in 10 of the cups, draw a set of large dots in the bottom of each for the numbers 1–5, drawing each set twice. Leave two cups blank for zero. Add the corresponding number of dried beans to the cups and then pour the contents into a zippered plastic bag for storage.

How to Play: Place the matching colors of beads or corresponding quantity of beans in the cups.

Sandpaper Numerals

To Play: Place a sheet of paper on a numeral. Hold a crayon lengthwise and rub it over the paper to see the shape. Do this again with other numerals.

Egg Carton Sort

To Play: Place the matching colors of beads or the right number of beans in the cups.

Math Box Activities

Number Bracelets

Packing the Math Box
- Beads
- Die with dots
- Chenille stem pieces

Getting Ready: Cut two 8 in. (20 cm) lengths of wire from chenille stems. Twist one end of each piece of fuzzy wire into a small ball so that beads will not slip off. Gather enough beads to make two bracelets and store them in a zippered plastic bag. You might wish to make multiple sets of materials for children to use.

How to Play: Work with a partner. Choose a piece of fuzzy wire. Roll a die and count the dots that are shown faceup. Then, add the corresponding number of beads to the fuzzy wire to begin a bracelet. Take turns rolling the die and adding beads to either one of the bracelets. Continue playing until both fuzzy wires are filled up with the same number of beads. Twist the ends together to complete each bracelet.

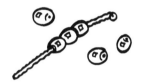

Number Wheel

Packing the Math Box
- Paper-plate number wheel
- Clothespins
- Die or pair of dice

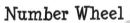

Getting Ready: Write the numerals 1–6 around the edges of a paper plate. To extend the activity, use numerals 1–12.

How to Play: Roll a die (dice) and count the dots that are shown faceup. Find the corresponding number on the paper plate and then mark it by attaching a clothespin. Continue playing until all numbers are marked with clothespins. (If playing with a partner, take turns rolling the dice and attaching a clothespin.)

Shape Sort

Packing the Math Box
- 6-cup muffin tin
- Shapes

Getting Ready: Cut several 2 in. (5 cm) or larger simple shapes (circles, triangles, squares, rectangles, ovals, etc.) out of foam or felt. Place all of the shapes in a large zippered plastic bag.

How to Play: Sort the shapes into the muffin tin cups so that all circles are in one of the cups, all squares are in another cup, all triangles are in a different cup, and so on.

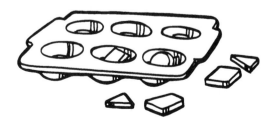

Math Box Activities

Fill 'n' Line Up Bottles ⭐

Packing the Math Box
- 5 empty bottles with lines drawn on them
- Paper towels for cleanup
- Squirt-top bottles filled with colored water

Getting Ready: Gather five clear-plastic water bottles. Using a bold-tip permanent marker, draw a line around each bottle as indicated: on bottle #1 about 1 in. (25 mm) from the bottom, on bottle #2 about 2 in. (5 cm) from the bottom, on bottle #3 about 3 in. (7 cm) from the bottom, and so on. Fill the squirt-top bottles with colored water.

How to Play: Fill each bottle up to the line with colored water from the squirt bottles. Then, put the bottles in order starting with the largest amount of water.

Little and Big Things ⭐

Packing the Math Box
- *Little* and *Big* printed on cards
- Assortment of paired little and big objects

Getting Ready: Gather an assortment of paired objects (two of each kind of item) for the concepts of "little" and "big." For example, you might find two balls—one that is very small in size and one that is larger. Other items may include two cars, two airplanes, and so on. Write the words *Little* and *Big* on index cards.

How to Play: Set the word cards on a table. Take the objects out of the box and match them by kind. Then, sort them by size. Put the smaller things near the word *Little* and larger things near the word *Big*. Gather other things from around the classroom that fit into the categories.

Candy Patterns ⭐

Packing the Math Box
- Pattern cards
- Candies

Getting Ready: Gather an assortment of wrapped candies such as mints or fruit-flavored chews. Separate the candies by kind and color and place them in piles. Using a hot glue gun, glue some pieces of candy onto index cards to create pattern cards. Keep the patterns simple. For example, an ABAB pattern card would be prepared by gluing a green mint, a red mint, a green mint, and then a red mint on the card. An ABC pattern card would include three different candies glued in order. Make several pattern cards. Store the extra pieces of candy in zippered plastic bags. Be sure there are enough pieces to extend the patterns you have created.

How to Play: Choose a pattern card. Using the provided candy, continue the sequence of the pattern off the card and onto the playing surface. Play again by extending other patterns shown on cards. Then, use the provided candy to create your own pattern.

Math Box Activities

Number Cups

Packing the Math Box

• Plastic cups
• Math counters

Getting Ready: Gather an assortment of plastic cups. Write the numerals 1–10 (or higher) individually on cups. Collect enough manipulatives (beans, interlocking cubes, small plastic people, large pasta shells, etc.) to make the corresponding sets of objects in the cups. Store the counters in a zippered plastic bag.

How to Play: Arrange the cups in the playing area. Look at the number on a cup. Fill the cup with the corresponding number of objects. Continue until all cups hold the correct amount of objects.

Marshmallow Toss

Packing the Math Box

• Numbered cartons
• Marshmallows

Getting Ready: Cut the tops off of 10 clean milk cartons. Write the numerals 1–10 individually on the cartons with a marker. Place 12–15 marshmallows in a zippered plastic bag.

How to Play: Arrange the cartons in order in a circle on the floor. To start the game, stand in the circle and toss a marshmallow into carton #1. Then, toss a marshmallow into carton #2. Continue in order until all cartons hold marshmallows.

Simple Scale Measuring

Packing the Math Box

• Simple scale or bucket balance
• Assorted items

Getting Ready: To create a simple balance scale, punch three holes 1/2 in. (13 mm) from each rim of two paper cups. Tie a 6 in. (15 cm) string through each hole. Gather all three strings from each cup and tie them to either end of a clothes hanger. Alternatively, have children use a manufactured bucket balance. Collect an assortment of items, such as crayons, blocks, rocks, socks, small plastic toys, etc., and place them in a large bag.

How to Play: Hang the hanger from a door knob or set the bucket balance on a hard surface. Choose an item from the bag and place it in a cup/bucket. Add an item to the other cup/bucket to see which item weighs more. Find out if it is possible to balance the two sides by placing items of similar weight in each cup/bucket.

Math Box Activities

Junk Drawer Measuring

Packing the Math Box
- Items to use as nonstandard measuring tools (several of each chosen item)
- Sticky-back note paper
- Pencil
- Pictures of classroom objects

Getting Ready: Take a digital photograph of several common objects in the classroom. Some examples might include a table, chair, rug, book, windowsill, counter, and sink. In the math box, place the pictures along with an assortment of items that you would find in a "junk drawer" to use as measuring tools. Be sure to include several of each chosen measuring tool so that children can place them lengthwise along one side of the object that is being measured. The tools could be identical plastic spoons, drinking straws, large paper clips, or pairs of shoelaces.

How to Play: Choose two pictures of classroom objects. Look at the first picture and find that object in the room. Measure it with the tools in the box. For example, if plastic spoons are the measuring tool, use them to find out the length of the chosen object. "How many spoons long is it?" Write the number of spoons counted on a sticky-back note and place it on the picture. Measure the second pictured item the same way. Compare the measurements.

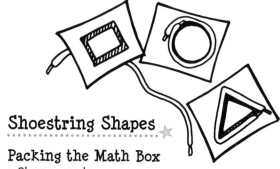

Shoestring Shapes

Packing the Math Box
- Shape cards
- Shoestrings

Getting Ready: To make the shape cards, cut card stock into large pieces. Draw a different geometric shape on each piece with a bold-tip marker. The shapes can include a circle, square, triangle, and rectangle. To challenge children, create cards that feature geometric shapes in different sizes.

How to Play: Choose an activity card and arrange a shoestring so that it covers the outline of the featured shape. Repeat the steps with the other shape cards.

Counting Bugs

Packing the Math Box

- 2 plastic bowls
- Plastic bugs
- Small aquarium net

Getting Ready: Fill the math box (or a plastic dishpan) two-thirds full of water. Place 10–12 plastic bugs in the water.

How to Play: Dip the net into the water and scoop up some bugs. Drop the bugs into a bowl. Place a second scoop of bugs into the other bowl. Count the bugs in each bowl. Dump the bowl with the most bugs back into the water and play again.

Number Bracelets

To Play: Find the fuzzy wires. Take turns rolling the die. Count the dots shown faceup. Add the correct number of beads to one of the wires. Play again and again to make bracelets.

Number Wheel

To Play: Roll the die or dice. Count the dots shown faceup. Find the matching number on the plate. Clip a clothespin on that number. Play until all numbers are marked.

Shape Sort

To Play: Sort the shapes into groups. Place all circles in one of the cups. Put the squares in another cup and so on.

Fill 'n' Line Up Bottles

To Play: Fill each bottle up to the line with water. Then, put the bottles in order starting with the largest amount of water.

Little and Big Things

To Play: Put the word cards on a table. First, match the objects by kind. Then, sort them by size and put each one near the correct word. Find other things in the room to sort.

Candy Patterns

To Play: Choose a candy pattern card. Use the wrapped candy to make the pattern shown. Play again with other cards. Then, make your own pattern.

Number Cups

To Play: Place the cups in order starting with the number 1. Read the numeral on a cup. Fill the cup with that number of objects. Play again by correctly filling the other cups.

Marshmallow Toss

To Play: Place the cartons in order in a circle. Stand in the middle of the circle. Toss a marshmallow into each carton in order. Play until all cartons hold marshmallows.

Simple Scale Measuring

To Play: Use the balance to measure things. Choose one item from the bag. Put it into one of the cups or buckets. Add items to the other cup or bucket to balance the scale. Play again.

Junk Drawer Measuring

To Play: Choose two pictures. Find the things in the room. Use the provided tools to measure them. Write each measurement on note paper and stick it to the picture.

Shoestring Shapes

To Play: Choose a card. Place a shoestring along the outline of the shape. Play again with another card.

Counting Bugs

To Play: Scoop up some bugs with the net. Drop them into the first bowl. Scoop up bugs again and drop them into the other bowl. Count the bugs. Dump the bowl with the most bugs back into the water. Play again.

File Folder Game — Bug Patterns

Materials

- file folder
- zippered plastic bag
- markers, scissors, and glue

Skill Builders

- patterning
- sort by kind

Extending the Lesson

Enlarge the bugs on page 26 and then copy them onto card stock. Cut out the bugs. Children can sort the bugs by kind into piles and then make their own patterns on a hard surface.

Getting Ready

1. Make a copy of this page and two copies of pages 25 and 26. Copy the pages on colored paper or use white paper and then color the scenes and individual bugs as desired. Cut out each bug separately. Cut out the "To Play" instruction box and the file-folder name tags found on this page.
2. Open the folder and orient it so that the tab is on the right. Glue a name tag onto the tab to identify the game.
3. Trim the copies of page 25 as desired. Then, glue the bug jars onto the panels of the file folder. Draw three heavy horizontal lines to divide the scene into four sections.
4. Choose two different kinds of bugs (two of each kind, four in total) and glue them in the first jar in the top section of the file folder in an ABAB pattern.
5. In the first jar on the left in the second section, create a different ABAB pattern by gluing four bugs in total, two of each kind. Continue by making patterns in the last two rows of jars.
6. After closing the folder, glue the "To Play" instruction box on the front panel.
7. Laminate the bug cards and trim around the edges (optional). Place them in a zippered plastic bag along with a ball of sticky-tack adhesive (optional). Tape a name tag to the front of the bag.
8. Optional: Laminate the entire file folder for durability. Trim around the edges.
9. Staple the plastic bag with bugs to the outside of the file folder.
10. Optional: Before children make patterns, show them how to use the sticky-tack adhesive to place the bugs in the jars.

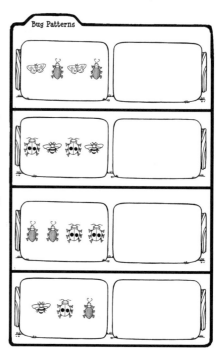

Bug Patterns

Bug Patterns

Bug Patterns

To Play

1. Take the bugs out of the bag.
2. Look at the bugs in the first jar.
3. Use bugs to make the second jar look the same.
4. Fill the other jars the same way.

Challenge: Use the bugs to make your own pattern. How many bugs are in the line?

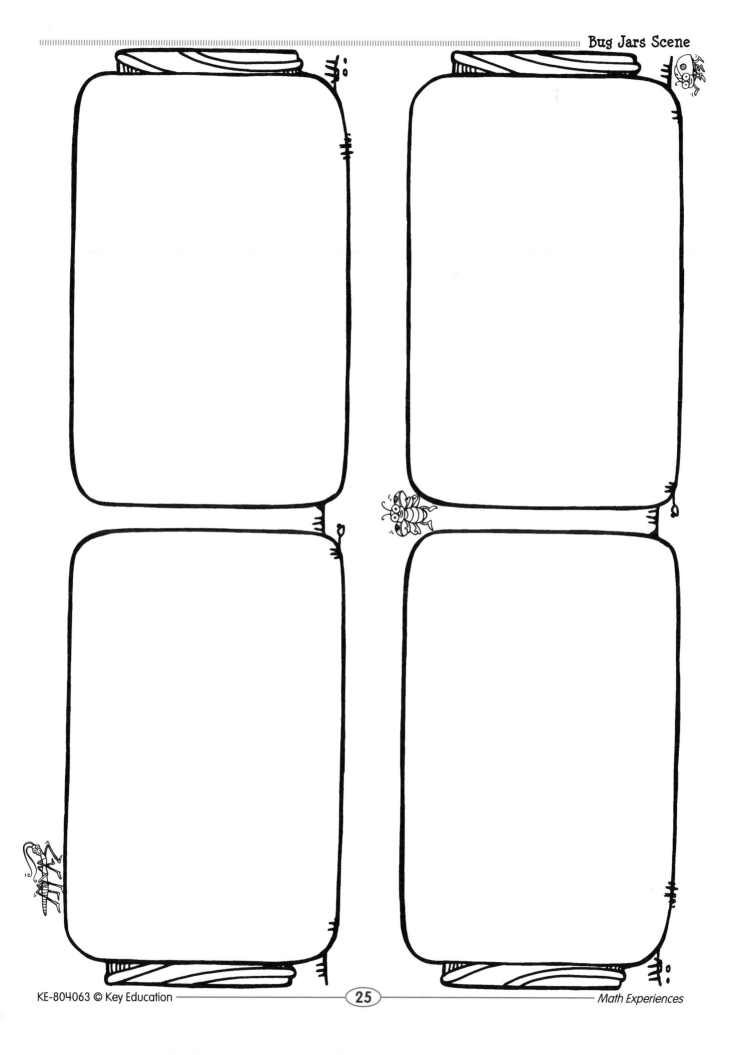

25

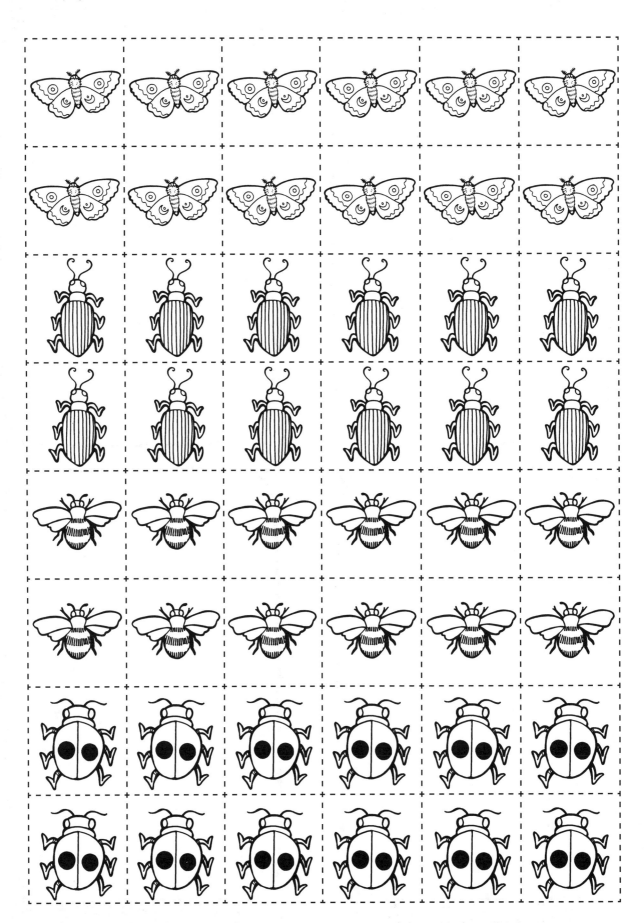

File Folder Game – Home Sweet Home

Materials

- file folder
- zippered plastic bag
- markers, scissors, tape, and glue
- index cards

Skill Builders

- sort and classify
- shape recognition

Extending the Lesson

Choose a few objects for children to sort by shape, such as beach ball—circle, flower box—square, sail on boat—triangle, and so on. Have children sort the objects on the back of the file folder.

Getting Ready

1. Make a copy of this page and the patterns on pages 28–31. Copy on colored paper or use white paper and then color the scenes and individual objects as desired. Cut out each object separately. Cut out the "To Play" instruction box and the file-folder name tags found on this page.
2. Laminate the objects and trim around the edges (optional). Place them in a zippered plastic bag along with a ball of sticky-tack adhesive (optional). Tape a name tag to the front of the bag.
3. Open the folder and orient it so that the tab is on the right. Glue a name tag onto the tab to identify the game.
4. Trim the copies of pages 28 and 29 as desired. Then, glue the house scene on the left panel and the yard scene on the right.
5. After closing the folder, glue the "To Play" instruction box on the front panel.
6. On the back panel of the closed folder, draw four simple shapes and boxes for sorting the objects into groups: circle, square, triangle, and rectangle.
7. Optional: Laminate the entire file folder for durability. Trim around the edges.
8. Staple the plastic bag with objects to the outside of the file folder.
9. Optional: Before children place the objects in the scenes, show them how to use the sticky-tack adhesive to arrange the objects on the file folder.
10. Prior to playing the game, have each child draw family members on two index cards. After coloring and cutting out the drawings, have the child place those family members in their favorite places in the house and yard.

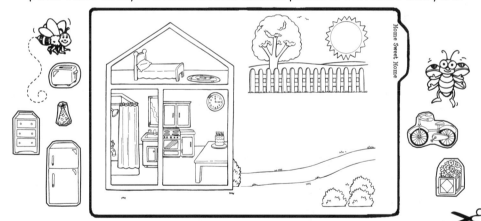

Home Sweet Home

Home Sweet Home

Home Sweet Home

To Play

1. Take the pieces out of the bag.
2. Look at the house and the yard.
3. Place each object in its proper location.
4. Place the drawings of family members in their favorite places in the scene.

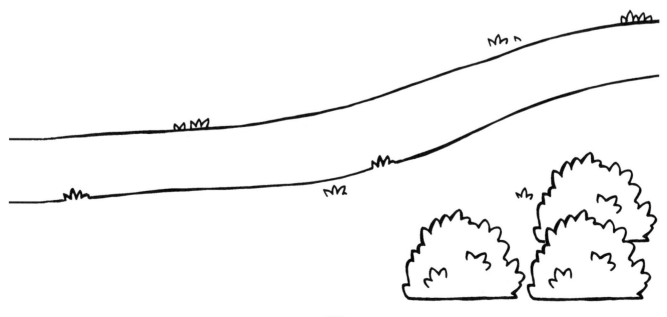

 Math Experiences

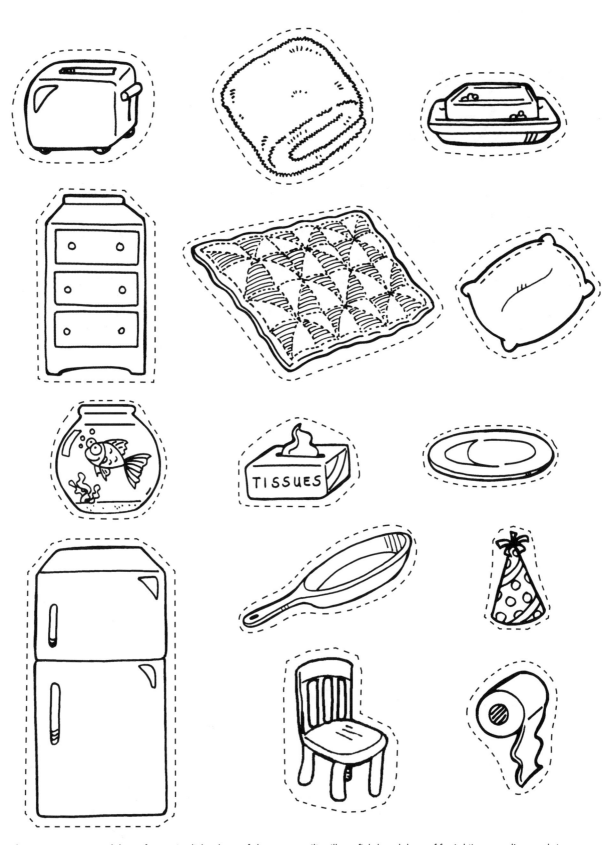

Pictures shown: toaster, towel, bar of soap in dish, chest of drawers, quilt, pillow, fish bowl, box of facial tissues, dinner plate, refrigerator, frying pan, party hat, chair, and bathroom tissue

Pictures shown: child's wading pool, ball, sidewalk chalk, sandbox, toy pail and shovel, bicycle, flower box, in-line skates, sailboat, toy box, and toilet

File Folder Game – Big or Little?

Materials

- colorful file folder
- zippered plastic bag
- markers, scissors, tape, and glue

Skill Builders

- sort and classify
- memory skills

Extending the Lesson

If children need additional practice comparing and sorting objects by size, see the math box activity "Little and Big Things" on page 20.

Getting Ready

1. Make a copy of this page and pages 33 and 34. Copy the pages on colored paper or use white paper and then color each animal individually as desired. Cut out each animal card along the dashed lines. Cut out the "To Play" instruction box and the file-folder name tags found on this page.
2. Laminate the animal cards and trim them around the edges (optional). Place them in a zippered plastic bag along with a ball of sticky-tack adhesive (optional). Tape a file-folder name tag to the front of the bag.
3. Open the folder and orient it so that the tab is on the right. Glue a name tag onto the tab to identify the game.
4. Using a bold-tip marker, write the word *Big* on the top of the left panel and the word *Little* on the top of the right panel.
5. After closing the folder, glue the "To Play" instruction box on the front panel.
6. Optional: Laminate the entire file folder for durability. Trim around the edges.
7. Staple the plastic bag with animal cards to the outside of the file folder.
8. Optional: Before children sort the cards, show them how to use the sticky-tack adhesive to place the animal cards on the file folder.

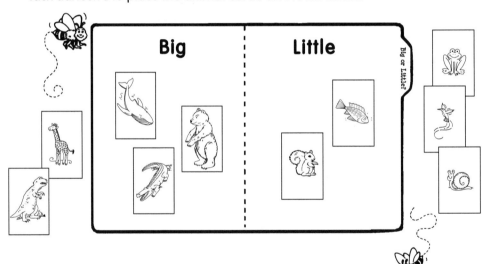

Big or Little?

Big or Little?

To Play

1. Take the animals out of the bag.
2. Choose one animal at a time. Decide if it is a "big" animal or a "little" animal.
3. Place the animal under the correct word.
4. Choose again until all animals are on the game board.

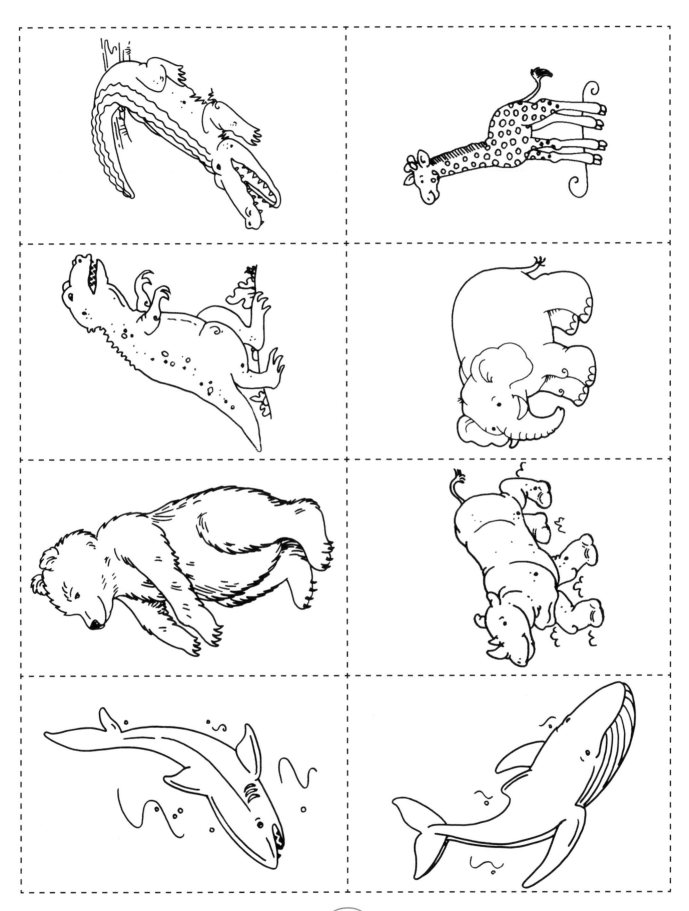

File Folder Game – Catching Bugs

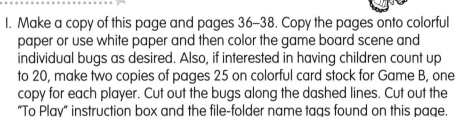

Materials

- 2 game markers
- colorful card stock
- colorful file folder
- standard die
- zippered plastic bag
- watercolor markers, scissors, tape, and glue

Skill Builders

- counting up to 10 or higher
- counting up to 20 and by 5s (Game B)

Getting Ready

1. Make a copy of this page and pages 36–38. Copy the pages onto colorful paper or use white paper and then color the game board scene and individual bugs as desired. Also, if interested in having children count up to 20, make two copies of pages 25 on colorful card stock for Game B, one copy for each player. Cut out the bugs along the dashed lines. Cut out the "To Play" instruction box and the file-folder name tags found on this page.
2. Laminate the bug cards and trim around the edges (optional). Place them in a zippered plastic bag. Tape a name tag to the front of the bag.
3. Open the folder and orient it so that the tab is on the right. Glue a name tag onto the tab to identify the game. Trim around the game board scene pieces as desired. Glue the two game board pieces to the file folder so that the borders overlap at the center of the fold, making the path one continuous loop through the garden.
4. For Games A and B, print the numerals 1–3 randomly on the stones.
5. After closing the folder, glue the "To Play" instruction box on the front panel.
6. Optional: Laminate the entire file folder and the bug jar mats (if playing Game B) for durability.
7. Staple the plastic bag with bugs to the outside of the folder.
8. For Game B, show the players how to place the collected bugs on their Bug Jar Mats, arranging only five bugs on each jar. The first player to collect 20 bugs altogether is the winner.

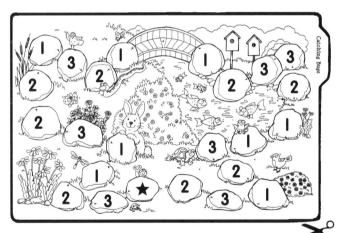

Catching Bugs

Catching Bugs

Catching Bugs

To Play (Partner Game)

Take the bugs out of the bag. Place your game marker on the ★. Take turns rolling the die and moving the same number of spaces as shown. Each time you stop on a stone, read the number and then collect the same number of bugs.

Game A: Go around the path once. Count your bugs.

Game B: Place the collected bugs in the jars on your mat. Only 5 bugs can be in each jar. The first player to "catch" 20 bugs altogether is the winner.

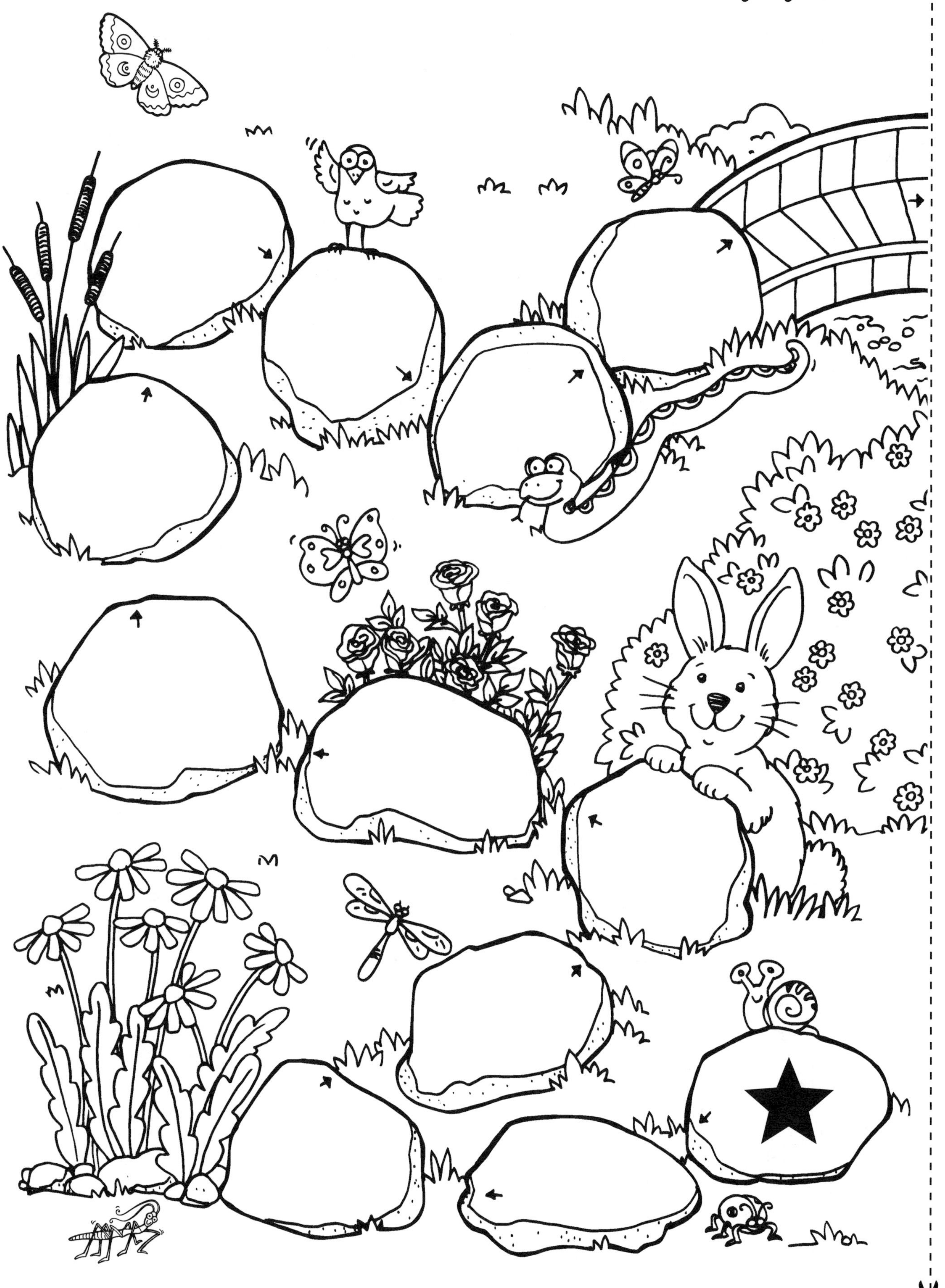

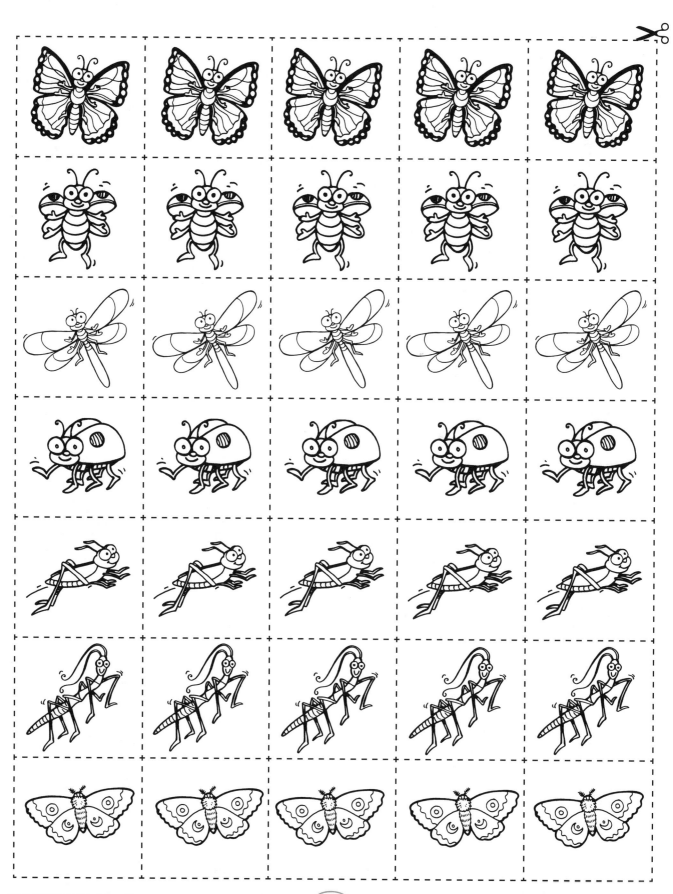

File Folder Game – Shape Factory

Materials

- file folder
- colorful card stock
- zippered plastic bag
- markers, scissors, tape, and glue

Skill Builders

- shape recognition
- one-to-one matching

Extending the Lesson

Have children make their own shape pictures on the file folder and then draw those figures in a little book. See pages 9 and 10 for book-making ideas.

Getting Ready

1. Make one copy of this page and the Shape Factory Scene pattern on page 40 and one copy of pages 42 and 43. Copy the pages on colored paper or use white paper and then color the Shape Factory Scene as desired. Make four or five copies of the shapes on page 41 on colorful card stock. Cut out each shape separately. Cut out the "To Play" instruction box and the file-folder name tags found on this page.
2. Laminate the shape pieces and trim around the edges (optional). Place them in a zippered plastic bag along with a ball of sticky-tack adhesive (optional). Tape a name tag to the front of the bag.
3. Open the folder and orient it so that the tab is on the right. Glue a name tag onto the tab to identify the game.
4. Trim around the factory scene as desired. Glue the scene on the left panel. Draw one star on the left panel. On the right panel, draw two stars and a large box to indicate where the shape picture will be made.
5. After closing the folder, glue the "To Play" instruction box on the front panel.
6. Optional: Laminate the entire file folder for durability. Trim around the edges.
7. Staple the plastic bag with shape pieces to the outside of the file folder.
8. Optional: Before children make pictures, show them how to use the sticky-tack adhesive to place the shapes in the factory scene.

Shape Factory / **Shape Factory**

To Play

1. Take the shapes out of the bag. Stack the picture cards. Place one card on the ★ box.
2. Use the shapes to make the same picture in the ★★ box.
3. Take off all pieces and play again with a new picture card.

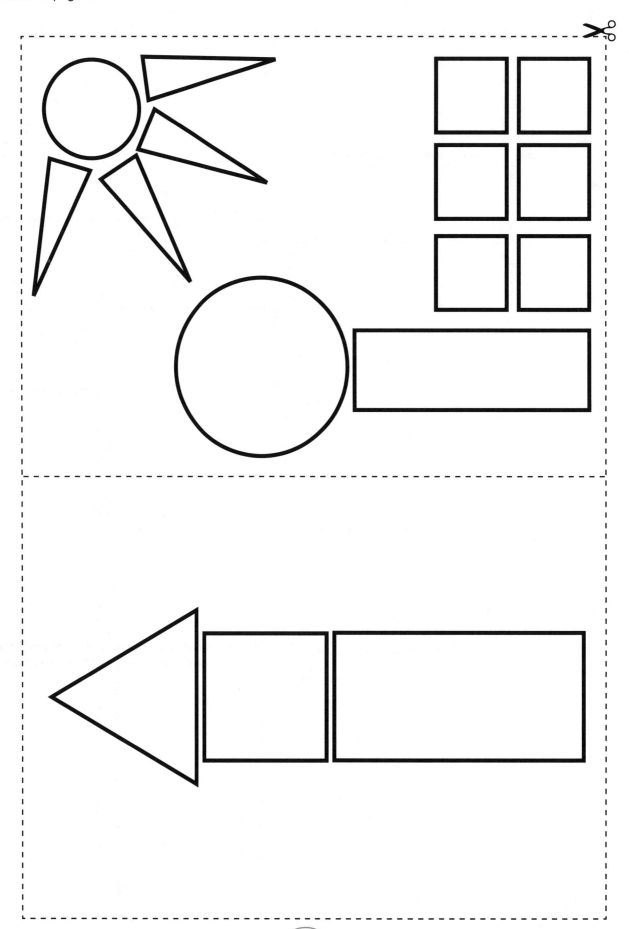

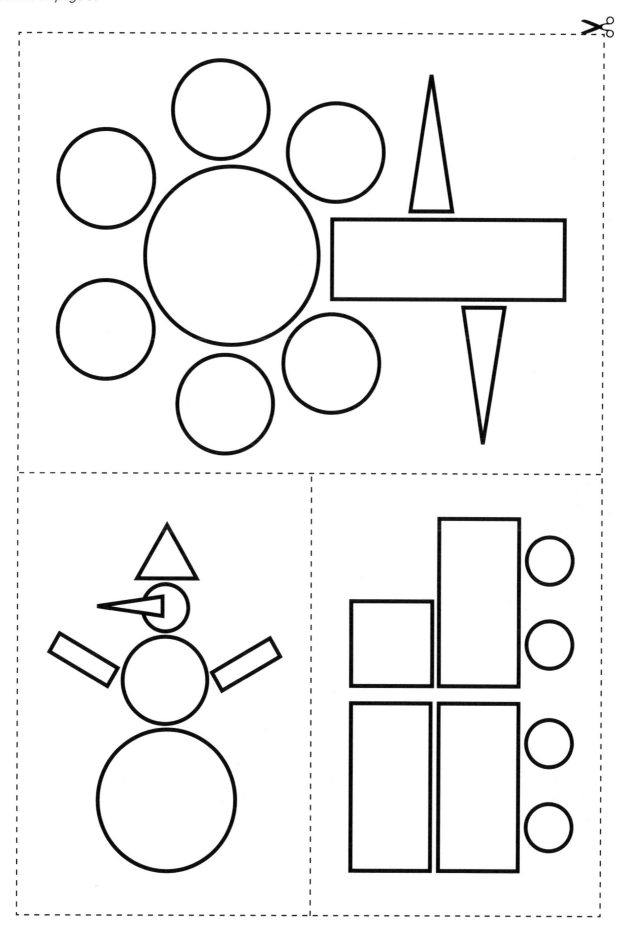

Sticks 'n' Stuff

Materials

- assortment of nature materials collected
- craft materials
- construction paper
- glue
- small boxes or buckets
- paper bags

Skill Builders

- patterning
- small-motor skills
- sorting and classifying

Getting Ready

- Gather an assortment of items from nature if you will not be able to collect them with children.

Extending the Lesson

- Have children create their own patterns. Provide them with an assortment of materials, such as cotton swabs, chenille stem pieces, buttons, small pom-poms, colored popcorn kernels, dried beans, various pasta shapes, and so on.

Activity

If your school is near a park or woodland, take children on an excursion to gather materials from nature. Give each child a bag and a suggestion of what to collect. Items might include small pebbles, sticks, leaves, pinecones, and acorns. *(Discourage children from picking flowers unless you are certain that those plants are not protected and there are numerous blossoms to ensure that the plant can reseed the area.)* If the school is not close to a park, encourage children to collect the materials over the weekend with their families, or you might wish to gather an assortment of nature items from a nearby park before presenting this activity.

During center time, have children sort the items into the provided boxes or buckets. Make sure there are enough containers so that each kind of leaf or item has its own box.

As a group, discuss how patterns are created by alternating two kinds of items over and over again. Demonstrate a simple pattern by having a few children line up in an ABAB pattern of boy/girl/boy/girl. Build another ABAB pattern by laying sticks and pebbles on the floor. To assess understanding of patterning, invite children to help you change the pattern on the floor to an AABB pattern or an ABC pattern.

To further the skill practice, give children sheets of construction paper. Have them create the demonstrated patterns on the paper with materials from nature. Be sure to examine the children's patterns before they glue on their pieces to ensure that they have actually created patterns. Once all the projects have dried, have children take turns explaining the patterns they created.

Science Connection: Patterns in Nature

When taking children on a nature walk, collect, photograph, or point out the many types of patterns that can be found in nature. Look at the parts of a pinecone, the stripes on a caterpillar, the petals on a flower, and so on. Alternatively, help children find manufactured patterns by noticing the arrangement of pavers in a walkway, breaks in a sidewalk, slats in a park bench, or stripes on their clothing.

Shark Attack

Materials

- 2 pieces of poster board
- bucket and water
- glue stick
- pictures of big and little things
- wooden skewers and masking tape
- lamination material
- empty dish detergent bottles
- *Smiley Shark* by Ruth Galloway

Skill Builders

- identifying numerals
- sorting and classifying

Getting Ready

- Clip an assortment of pictures of big and little things from magazines.
- Make 10 copies of the shark on page 46 on card stock for the game Shark Attack. Write a numeral 1–10 on each shark. Laminate the sharks and trim about $\frac{1}{8}$" (3 mm) around each shape. Tape a wooden skewer to the back of each shark and then poke the skewers into the ground in a large, open, grassy area.
- Fill the dish detergent bottles and bucket with water.

Extending the Lesson

To play Shark Attack, have children sit in a line on the side of a grassy area. Call out a child's name and a number. The chosen child dashes to the shark with the corresponding numeral and squirts it with water from a detergent bottle. Continue until all children have played.

Activity

Begin the lesson by talking about the differences in sizes between a shark and a small fish. If interested, have children use their bodies to show the length of a shark. (The great hammerhead shark can reach a length of 18 ft. [5.5 m].) Read aloud *Smiley Shark* by Ruth Galloway (Magi Publications, 2006). Have children discuss their ideas about the book. Also, point out that the word *big* does not necessarily mean *scary* or *mean*.

Chant the rhyme below, using your fingers to show numbers.

Five Little Fish

Five little fish swam 'round and 'round
All on a bright summer day.
When a great big fish went "chomp,"
   "chomp," "chomp,"
One little fish swam away.

Repeat other verses: **Four** little fish . . . ,
Three little fish . . . , and **Two** little fish . . .

One little fish swam 'round and 'round
All on a bright summer day.
When the great big fish went "chomp,"
   "chomp," "chomp,"
That little fish did not swim away.
He looked that great big fish right in the eye
And said, "That's not how we play!"
"Stop that chomp, chomp, chomping right now!"
And the great big fish said, "Okay!"

Assess what children have learned about the concepts of big and little by having them sort pictures. Let each child choose one or two pictures from your collection and then place them in the corresponding piles. When finished, label one sheet of poster board with the word *Big* and the other poster board with the word *Little*. Glue the pictures in the proper categories on the poster boards.

Large Motor Connection: Tagging Minnows

Choose one child to be the "shark." Invite the other children to be the "minnows." In a large playing area, have the minnows spread out away from the shark. At your signal, all the minnows begin "swimming" around the "ocean" to prevent being tagged by the shark. If the shark does tag a minnow, that fish also becomes a shark. Continue the game until all players have become sharks.

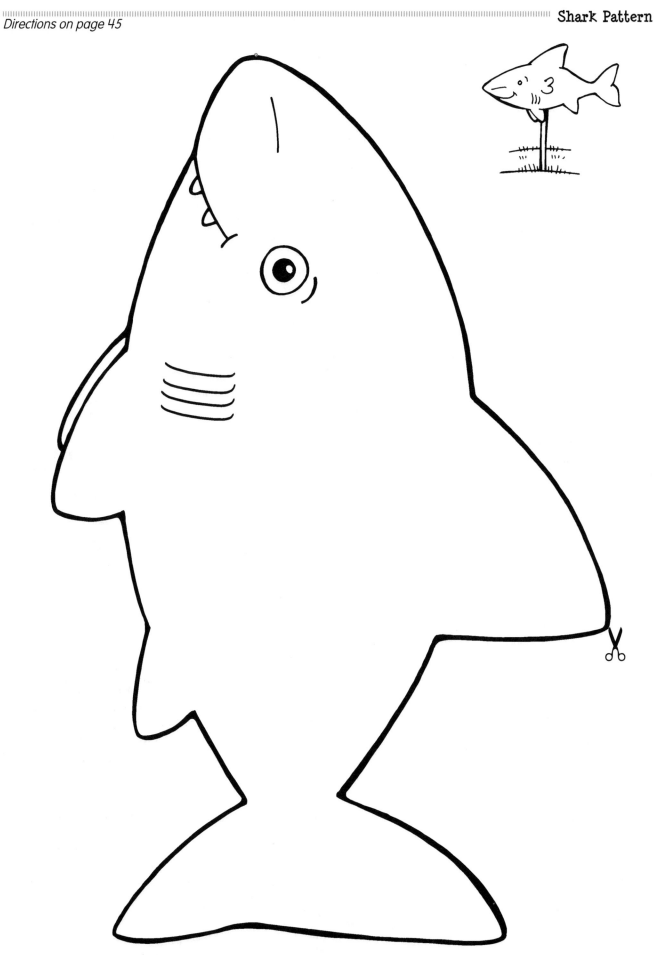

46

Shape Stretch

Materials

- CD player and music
- elastic
- crayons and paper
- craft sticks and tape
- poster board and scissors
- *When a Line Bends . . . A Shape Begins* by Rhonda Gowler Greene
- *Round Is a Mooncake: A Book of Shapes* by Roseanne Thong or *Shapes, Shapes, Shapes* by Tana Hoban

Skill Builders

- shape recognition

Getting Ready

- Cut a piece of elastic, purchased at a fabric or craft store, into 4 ft. (1.25 m) lengths, one for each child. Tie the ends together securely in a knot. Make a larger piece for yourself. You should be able to stretch the elastic to hold both hands over your head while standing on the other end of the elastic loop.
- Make enlarged copies of the shape cards on page 48. Cut them out along the dashed lines. Tape each shape to a craft stick to make a sign.

Extending the Lesson

Read *The Shape of Me and Other Stuff* by Dr. Seuss (Random House, 1973). Then, give each child a shape card. Let children find something in the classroom that has that featured shape.

Activity

Hold up one of the shape signs, such as the rectangle, and then have children identify it. Ask them if there is anything else they can tell you about the shape. Count the sides and talk about how we distinguish shapes by their unique features. *(Note: The pentagon and octagon are provided only for counting the sides of those shapes and are a lot of fun for children to make by working cooperatively with others.)* Read *When a Line Bends . . . A Shape Begins* by Rhonda Gowler Greene (Houghton Mifflin, 2001). Have children look for the different shapes in the book. Then, let them practice turning lines into shapes with crayons on paper.

Making shapes with an elastic loop can be a lot of fun. Hand out the elastic loops and then direct children to step on their loops with their feet and then stretch the elastic over their heads. Demonstrate with your loop how to make a rectangle with the elastic by evenly spreading out the legs and arms. Let children practice making triangles and rectangles with the elastic loops. If making the shape with their bodies is too difficult, direct children to work with partners to make the shape.

Continue the activity with more difficult shapes by having children pair off to make the rhombus, circle, oval, and square; form groups of five members for making the pentagon; and work in groups of eight members for the octagon.

Finally, play a favorite piece of music (soft, flowing music rather than loud, jazzy songs may work best for this activity). Hold up one of the shape signs and have children explore ways to create the shape.

Literacy Connection: Shape Books

Read *Round Is a Mooncake: A Book of Shapes* by Roseanne Thong (Chronicle, 2000) or *Shapes, Shapes, Shapes* by Tana Hoban (Greenwillow, 1986). Talk about the different shapes that can be found all around us. Make a simple little book for each child by stapling a few half sheets of copy paper together or refer to pages 9 and 10 for other book-making ideas. Have children write about and draw pictures of their favorite shapes and the things that have those shapes in their little books.

Take Me Out to the Ball Game

Materials

- 10 old T-shirts and a roll of painter's tape
- 20 clothespins
- rope
- baseball/softball
- small rubber balls
- index cards
- safety pins
- large sheets of paper and markers
- baseball clip art or stickers

Skill Builders

- number recognition 1–10
- number sequence
- small motor skills

Getting Ready

- Write the numerals 1–10 individually on small index cards. Make two sets. You will also need to make duplicate cards if there are more than 10 children in your class. Decorate the cards as desired with baseball clip art or stickers.
- Tape the second set of number cards in a circle on the floor.
- Collect an assortment of baseball or sports shirts featuring numbers 1–10. Alternatively, create your own number T-shirts by forming numerals with wide pieces of tape on the backs of several shirts.
- String a long length of rope across the classroom to make a clothesline.

Activity

At the beginning of circle time, sing a few phrases of the song "Take Me Out to the Ball Game" if you know it. Then, hand each child a number card. Explain that these cards are their "tickets." Each child must find a place to sit by matching the numeral on the card to the same numeral on the floor.

Once everyone is seated, begin by rolling a baseball or softball to a child. Have that child roll the ball back to you and say "one." Then, roll the ball to the second child who in turn counts "one, two." The third child who receives the ball will count "one, two, three" and so on.

After all children have had a chance to roll the ball back to you, give each child a number T-shirt. Explain that you have a new baseball team and that you need to distribute the team jerseys to the players. The shirts must be arranged in order so that the players can find their numbers. Begin by having the child who is holding the T-shirt with the lowest number hang the shirt on the clothesline. Continue until all shirts are hanging in numerical order.

Extending the Lesson

For additional practice in sequencing numbers, leave off the numerals on one or two of the T-shirts. Hang the shirts on the line in random order. Have children work in small groups to rearrange the T-shirts in numerical order and write the missing numerals on large sheets of paper. Help them use safety pins to attach the papers to the blank shirts.

Alternatively, the children may work with numbers 1–12, 1–15, 1–20, or another range of numbers.

Gross Motor Connection: Number Shoot

Hang the clothesline and the T-shirts outside. Mark a line a short distance back from the shirts. Let children toss small rubber balls the corresponding number of times at the shirts. For example, throw the ball once to hit the shirt with the numeral 1, throw the ball twice at the shirt with the numeral 2, and so on.

Find Me First

Materials

- photographs of classroom objects
- chenille stems
- construction paper
- dried chickpeas or small white lentils
- index cards
- marker, scissors, glue, and paper cutter
- tissue paper
- book on butterflies

Skill Builders

- ordinal numbers
- memory
- matching

Getting Ready

- Using a digital camera, take photos of small common objects in the classroom, such as a chair, an assortment of toys, craft tools, pillows, etc.
- Write the numerals 1, 2, and 3 individually on index cards.
- Fold the construction paper into thirds. Write the word *First* in the first section, *Middle/ Second* in the second section, and *Last/Third* in the third section.
- Cut the chenille stems into smaller pieces.
- Cut the tissue paper into 6 in. (15 cm) squares.
- Cut several leaf shapes out of green construction paper, one for each child.

Activity

If your preschoolers/kindergartners do not understand the words *first, middle,* and *last,* choose three children to come to the front of the class and give each child a number card. Ask the selected children to arrange themselves in numerical order. Let the class count the children who are holding the cards. Ask the class to tell you which child is standing in the *middle.* Next have them identify who is *first* and who is *last* in the small group. (If appropriate, introduce the ordinal words; *first, second,* and *third.*) Continue the lesson until all children have had an opportunity to hold and arrange number cards.

To extend the lesson, change the activity into a scavenger hunt. Choose three new children to come forward. Give each selected child a picture of an object in the classroom. Direct those children to find the objects that match the pictures and bring them back to the group. As the children return to the group, place their pictures in a row to show the order in which they arrived. Have children put the found objects in the same order.

Science Connection: Butterfly Life Stages

The butterfly's life cycle has very definite stages. All butterflies begin their lives inside tiny eggs before hatching as caterpillars. After spending several weeks as a little "feeding machine," each caterpillar "rests" inside a special case known as a chrysalis while its body changes in shape. Finally, it emerges as a beautiful butterfly. *(Note: This explanation has been simplified for young learners.)* As a class, read aloud a favorite book on butterflies that shows realistic pictures of the first stage (egg), second stage (caterpillar), and third stage (adult butterfly).

Give each child a sheet of construction paper that has been folded and labeled. To represent the first stage of a butterfly's life, have the child glue a leaf shape in the first panel and a small dried lentil on the leaf as the "egg." Next, let the child twist two chenille stems together to create a "caterpillar" and glue it in the second panel. Finally, for the third panel, direct the child to gather a piece of tissue paper down the center, twist a chenille stem around the middle to create a "butterfly," and glue it in place.

Boxes, Boxes, Boxes

Materials

- 3 different-sized cardboard boxes
- assorted objects in various sizes
- small stuffed bear

Skill Builders

- following directions
- relative position of objects
- size relationships

Extending the Lesson

Turn a large box on its side so that the opening is facing away from the children. Place all the sorting items in a bag next to the large box. Have one child select an item from the bag and hide it in the overturned box. Let the child describe the item first by size and then by offering other details about the object until the class guesses what is hidden in the box. Repeat until all the objects have been described.

Activity

After locating one large-, one medium-, and one small-sized box, gather a selection of objects that best fits inside of each of the boxes. Set the items in a group off to the side.

Pick up one of the boxes and ask a child to select an object that best fits inside of that box. When all the children have had a chance to choose an object that fits inside of a box, talk about their decisions. Demonstrate the fact that little things will fit inside of boxes that are bigger than they are; however big things will not fit inside of boxes that are smaller than they are. Have children search for other objects in the classroom that fit inside of selected boxes.

Set the largest box in front of the class. Tell children that you are going to play the game "Bear, Can You Do This?" to see how "smart" the teddy bear is. Explain that you will give Bear a task, but he will need the children's help to follow the directions. Choose one child to come forward and hold the teddy bear. Give a direction, such as "Bear, sit on the box." (The child would then place the bear on top of the box.) Select another child and give a different command. Call out various directions to use the words *in, out, over, under, in front of, behind, around,* and so on. As

children become proficient with the task, challenge them with two- or three-step instructions to complete.

Large-Motor Connection: "Jack" Be Nimble

How "nimble" can children be to follow specific directions? To find out, place a large-, a medium-, and a small-sized box on the floor in the middle of the group of children. Choose one child to come forward. Chant the nursery rhyme, "Jack Be Nimble," replacing "Jack" with the child's name and stating the positional command and box description. Say, for example, "Derek be nimble. Derek be quick. Derek jump over the medium-sized box." Vary the directions for each child. Ideas include "stand under the largest box," "run around the smallest box," and so on.

How Many Steps?

Materials

- card stock
- identical blocks and other identical objects to use as measuring tools
- masking tape
- paper bags and poster board
- marker, scissors, and glue
- small, sticky-back note paper
- simple scale and a bucket balance
- various items to measure
- *The Line Up Book* by Marisabina Russo

Skill Builders

- measuring distance and weight
- cooperation

Getting Ready

- Make two copies of page 53 on card stock. Cut out the cards along the dashed lines.
- Create a chart by gluing one set of cards along the left side of a sheet of poster board. Divide the remaining space on the poster in half by drawing a vertical line. At the top of the first column write *Guess*. Above the second column write *Count*.
- Mark a large **X** on the floor with masking tape.
- Fill several paper bags with identical objects to use as measuring tools.
- Place several items to be measured in a paper bag and then set those materials along with a simple scale and a bucket balance in the science center.

Activity

Have children sit around the large **X** on the floor. Read aloud *The Line Up Book* by Marisabina Russo (Greenwillow, 1986). Talk about all the things that Sam lines up in each room to measure his way back to the kitchen. Count each of the objects he adds to his line. After the book discussion, introduce the picture cards and let children identify the location of each one. Explain that they will measure the distance from the **X** to the place shown on each card. Then, encourage children to estimate the number of steps for each distance. Write down a few of the children's estimates on the poster by the corresponding pictures.

Divide the class into teams of two or three players. Give each team a card, a sticky-back note paper, and a pencil. Starting on the **X**, have children count their steps while walking to the locations indicated on their cards. (You will need to do this as a group with very young children.) Have them record the number of steps taken on their note paper. When children have finished counting their steps, they should return to the poster and place their note papers in the second column next to the matching picture card. Once all teams are finished, compare the guesses to the actual number of steps taken for the measurements.

Alternatively, give each team a bag with identical measuring "tools" inside. Show how to "line up" the measuring tools to find out how far it is from the **X** on the floor to a selected location.

Science Connection: Guess and Measure

In the science center, encourage children to learn about another way to measure things. Pair off children and have them take turns removing an item from the bag. Children can compare the two items and identify the one that is heavier (or lighter). They may use a bucket balance to find out if they were correct. If appropriate, also let them guess how much each item weighs and then place it on a simple scale to measure its actual weight. Compare the guesses to the actual measured weights. Repeat the steps until all objects in the bag have been weighed.

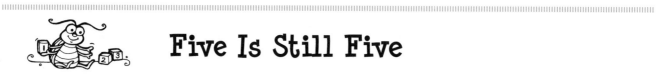

Five Is Still Five

Materials

- collage materials (craft items, pictures clipped from magazines, etc.)
- construction paper
- glue and scissors
- masking tape
- paper bags

Skill Builders

- number permanence
- one-to-one correspondence

Getting Ready

- Use masking tape to make a circle 2 ft. (61 cm) in diameter on the floor for each child.
- For extending the lesson, place various quantities of objects in paper bags. For example, one bag may hold a few items and other bags may have sets up to 10 or higher.

Extending the Lesson

Place the bags holding sets of objects on a table. Children can count the objects in each bag. Alternatively, let children sort all of the objects in a different way and then recount to verify the number in each bag. It is also possible to challenge children by having them match bags with sets of equivalent values or direct them to find two bags that equal the quantity of objects in a third bag.

Activity

Does the number of things change if the objects are rearranged? Explore this concept with young preschoolers. Invite them to count the fingers and thumb on one of their hands while touching them individually. Then, have children turn their hands upside down and recount their fingers and thumbs. No matter which direction they hold their hands, the number of fingers on each hand will always be *five*.

Repeat the same activity by using children as the objects to be counted. Rearrange the group of five children in various ways and have the class recount them each time.

Finish the lesson by letting children conduct a "Number Hunt" in the classroom. To do this, give each child a paper bag for collecting five things and then send them out to find their objects. When they return, have each child select a taped circle on the floor and place the collected objects inside it. Encourage children to count their objects in the circles by touching each one as they say a number word. Next, direct children to arrange their objects in rows inside their circles and then count the objects again. Continue the investigation by having children regroup their objects in vertical lines, arrange them close together as bunches, place them around the perimeters of their circles, and so on. Each time the objects are rearranged, let children count them and then call out the number. Be sure to point out that no matter how the objects are arranged, the number of objects is always the same.

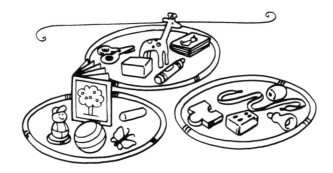

Fine-Motor Connection: A Collage of 5s

Place an assortment of collage items in separate containers. Let children decide what they would like to use to make their collages. As they choose various items, they must gather five of each kind of item. (Remind children to count their items carefully.) Let them place five dots of glue on sheets of construction paper and then place each craft material on a dot of glue. Have children continue adding more items in sets of five to finish their collages.

Snack Time Math

Materials

- paper plates, plastic spoons, plastic knives
- bread and jelly or jam
- paper bags
- items for classroom deli
- *Two Greedy Bears* by Mirra Ginsburg
- *Eating Fractions* by Bruce McMillan

Skill Builders

- dividing things in half
- one-to-one correspondence
- patterning

Extending the Lesson

- Each day, provide an opportunity to explore math at snack time. Split whole graham crackers in half and then in half again. Cut a piece of fruit in half and have the children count seeds. Pull an orange apart and count the sections. Count how many bites it takes to eat the snack.
- Have children create patterns on paper plates with an assortment of crackers or dry cereal before eating the food.
- Pair off children and give each team its snack on a plate. Let children count the items on the plate and then figure out how many crackers or cookies each will receive before picking up the food and eating it.

Activity

Have the children sit in a circle and read aloud *Two Greedy Bears* by Mirra Ginsburg (Aladdin, 1998). Discuss how the two quarrelsome friends could not decide on who was hungrier or who should have more and how the fox outwitted the two bears and ate their lunch. You may prefer to read aloud the book *Eating Fractions* by Bruce McMillan (Scholastic, 1991) and then talk about dividing something in half and sharing it with a friend. This could be demonstrated, for example, if you planned to serve jelly on bread during snack time. Spread some jelly on a piece of bread and then ask children to suggest what you could do if you and a friend both want the slice of bread. Show children how to divide the bread by cutting it in half. Have the class form teams of two children. Give each team one plate, one slice of bread, a small cup of jelly and a spoon, and a plastic knife. After children have washed their hands, let members of each team take turns spreading some jelly on a slice of bread. Generate ideas about what they could do so that both team members may have some jelly on bread. Talk about estimating *half* of something. After the bread is cut in half, allow children time to enjoy their open-faced sandwiches. Repeat the activity by distributing another slice of bread to each team. Alternatively, have children make their own jelly sandwiches to cut in half and eat.

Dramatic-Play Connection: Classroom Deli

Create a classroom deli by providing an assortment of lunch items such as "sandwiches" (consisting of two slices of bread in a plastic bag sealed with tape), small apples and bananas (real or plastic), juice boxes, small bags of chips, napkins, plastic plates, and so on. Provide a small table and chairs, a table for a deli counter, a cash register, play money, a billfold for customer to use, and a menu. After setting up the deli, explain to children that they need to pack "lunches" to sell. Each lunch must contain one of each predetermined item for each "customer." Help them figure out how many cents each sandwich and other food items will cost and then make signs on poster boards. When they are finished with the preparations, open their deli for business.

Match My Size

Materials

- 2 cardboard boxes
- assorted objects from classroom
- craft paper and rope
- markers and scissors
- ingredients for "Yummy Toppings" activity

Skill Builders

- measurement
- size relationships

Get Ready

- Gather an assortment of objects from around the classroom. Place the items in a large box. Make a second collection of objects in another box.
- Cut a piece of rope into varied lengths—from about 3 in. (8 cm) to 2 ft. (61 cm) in length.
- Cut a piece of craft paper into 3 ft. (91 cm) strips, one for each child.

Extending the Lesson

Place the pieces of rope in the middle of the table. Give each child a strip of craft paper and a marker. Have children choose a piece of rope. After looking at their rope pieces, let them try to draw lines on the paper about as long as their ropes. When finished, direct children to lay their pieces of rope along their drawn lines to compare lengths. Then, invite them to find objects that are similar in length to the selected pieces of rope.

Activity

Have children sit in a circle. Choose one child to select an item from the box. Then, give that child a direction to find another item in the room. Say, "Look for something that is [similar, smaller, or larger] in size." For example, after Pearl chooses a small stuffed animal from the bag, you might tell her to find something in the room that is the same size as the chosen animal. Continue in this manner until everyone has collected an object.

When everyone is holding a "found" object, explain how to play a new game called "Trade In." Set the second box of collected objects in the center of the group. Choose a child to be the player by "trading in" the found object for one in the box. The player must tell you if the new object should be bigger or smaller than the found object. Pull out an item that corresponds to what size trade-in the player asked for. Have fun with this activity. At times, pull out an object from the box that is not the correct size and assess if the child catches the "error."

Cooking Connection: Yummy Toppings

Here is a tasty way to compare the sizes of sweet treats! For each child, spread frosting on a sugar cookie and then add some sprinkles on top of the frosting. Have the child choose the topping that is a little bit "bigger than" the sprinkles. Continue by adding two or three more yummy toppings, such as jelly beans and chewy bear shapes. Just remember that the toppings in each layer should be a little bit bigger than the toppings in the layer under them. Enjoy!

Go Fish and More Card Games

Materials

- 3 zippered plastic bags
- colorful card stock
- markers, tape, and scissors

Skill Builders

- one-to-one matching
- matching numerals to sets of objects that they represent

Getting Ready ★

General Directions: Make a copy of this page on colorful paper. Cut out the game name tags and the "To Play" instruction box from this page.

Match Up Numbers Games

1. Copy the cards on pages 58–62 onto colorful card stock. Cut out the cards along the dashed lines.
2. Laminate the cards for durability and trim around the edges (optional). Sort the cards into two groups. For Set 1, place the cards that feature animals and plants along with the numerals in a zippered plastic bag. For Set 2, place the cards showing sets of stars along with the cards that show fingers extended in a different zippered plastic bag. Tape the corresponding game name tag to the front of each bag.

Go Fish for Numbers! Game

1. Copy the cards on pages 58–62 onto colorful card stock. Cut out the cards along the dashed lines.
2. Laminate the cards for durability and trim around the edges (optional). Place the deck of cards in a zippered plastic bag. Tape the game name tag and the "To Play" instruction box to the front of the bag.

Match Up Numbers

Match Up Numbers

Go Fish for Numbers!

Go Fish for Numbers!

To Play (Game for Three Players)

1. Shuffle the cards.

2. Deal six cards to each player. Place the remaining cards facedown in a stack. All players look at their cards and lay down sets of two or four cards that stand for the same number.

3. Choose a player to start the game.

4. Player A looks at the cards in his hand and then asks one of the other players "Do you have any cards that show [say the number]? (The requested number must match one of the cards that Player A is holding.) If the player is holding a card that matches the requested number, the card is given to Player A. Player A then lays down that set and asks one of the players for a different number card. If the player is not holding the requested card, that player says "Go Fish for Numbers!" Player A then draws a card from the deck to finish the turn. Player B now takes a turn.

5. Continue playing the game in the same manner until all of the cards have been used to make sets. The player who collects the most cards is declared the winner.

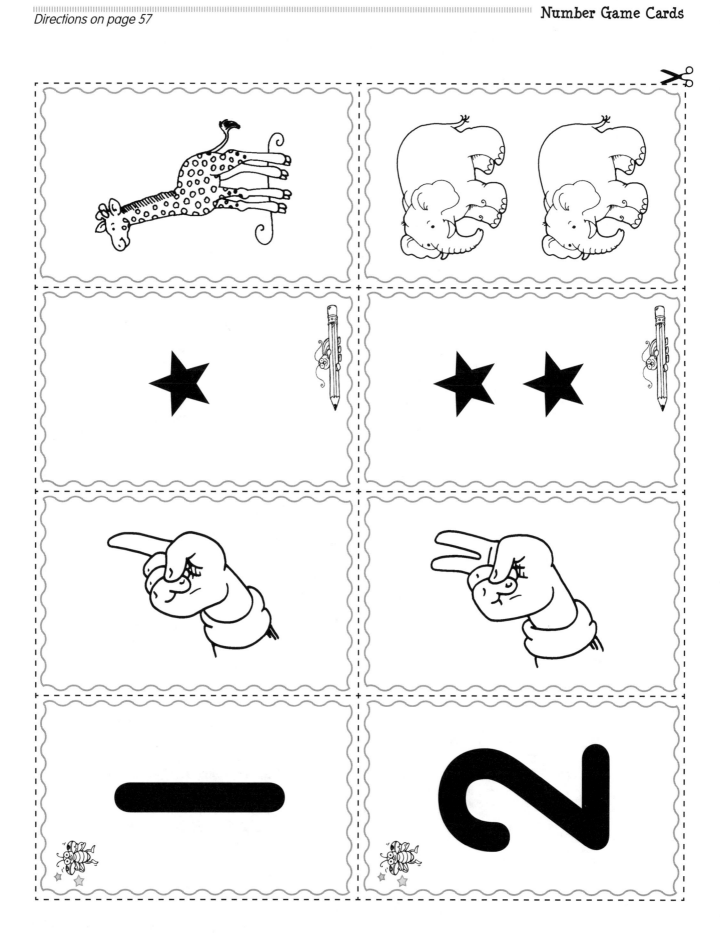

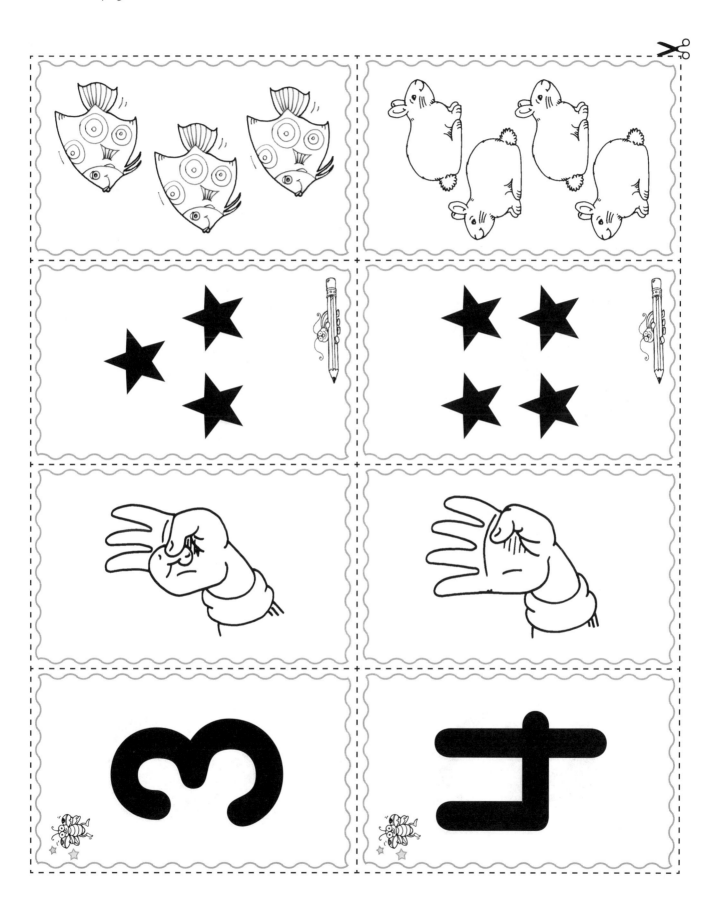

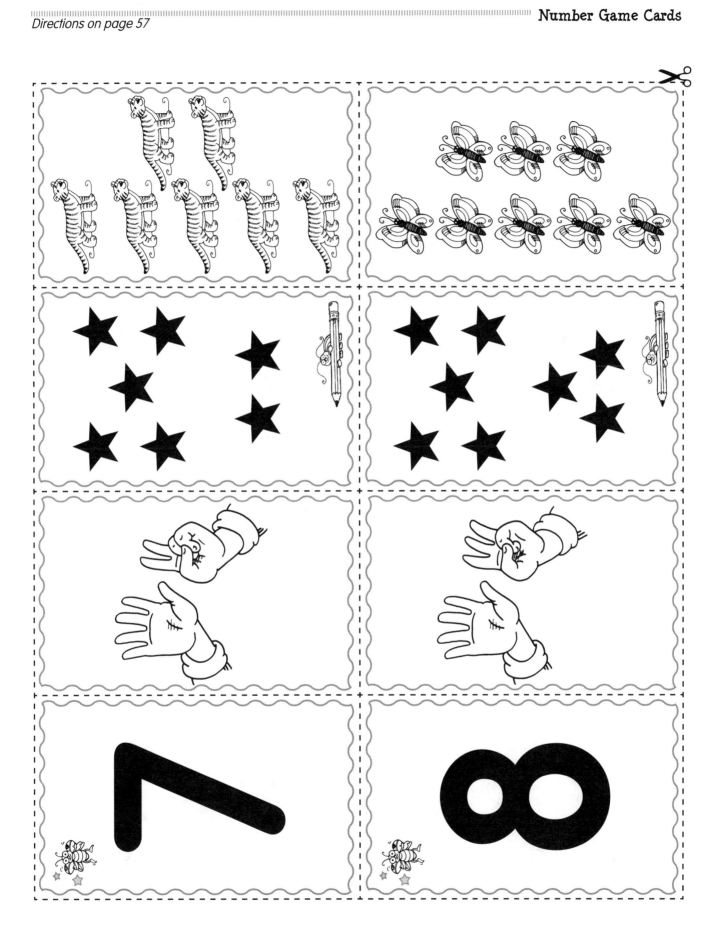

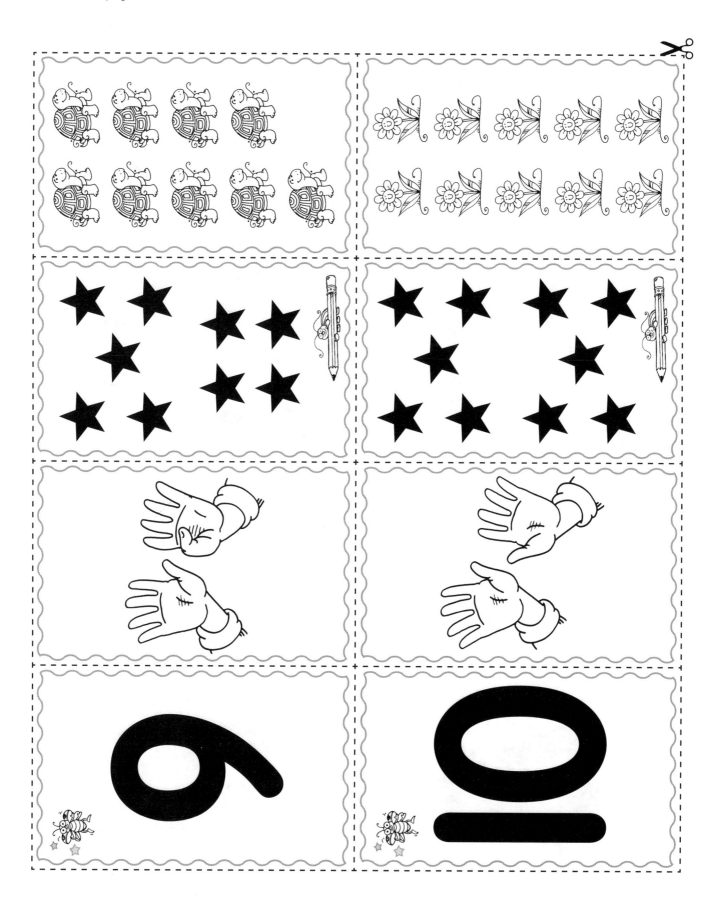

Correlations to Position Statement

Math Experiences for Young Learners supports the following recommendations for classroom practice from *Early Childhood Mathematics: Promoting Good Beginnings*, a joint position statement of the National Association for the Education of Young Children (NAEYC) and the National Council for Teachers of Mathematics (NCTM).

1. Teachers should support children's natural interest in mathematics and their tendency to use it to learn about their world.
   The activities in this book build upon children's natural curiosity in mathematics by integrating mathematics concepts into a wide variety of activities, from individual play to partner games to large-group activities.

2. Teachers should use children's prior experiences, background knowledge, and individual learning styles as a basis for teaching mathematics.
   The activities in this book draw on students' prior experiences and background knowledge by using concepts and materials with which they are familiar and by promoting family involvement in mathematics learning. The many different types of activities support many different student learning styles.

3. Teachers should base their mathematics curriculum and teaching on what they know about all aspects of child development.
   The introductory material on concept development stages and the suggested activities make it clear how the book supports developmentally appropriate practices by emphasizing hands-on work at the right level for children.

4. Teachers should use mathematics curriculum and teaching methods that strengthen children's abilities in all areas of mathematics skills, including problem-solving, reasoning, representing, communicating, and connecting mathematical ideas.
   This book offers open-ended problem solving activities, along with activities such as games, group discussions, and mini-books that enable students to build skills in all of these mathematical areas.

5. Teachers should be sure that early childhood mathematics curriculum supports important "big ideas" in later mathematics.
   The activities build a basis for all of the major areas of mathematics in the primary grades.

6. Teachers should provide students with in-depth interaction with important mathematical ideas. In early childhood, key areas of study include number and operations, geometry, measurement, and patterning.
   This book provides for in-depth exploration of ideas in the areas of number and operations, geometry, measurement, and sorting and patterning. Each area has a variety of activities associated with it, presented in a variety of ways.

7. Teachers should integrate mathematics into the curriculum, teaching it in conjunction with other subject areas.
   The activities in this book integrate explicitly, not only into other curriculum areas, but also into everyday classroom routines like lining up or center time. Many activities include explicit instructions for integration, including integrated literature suggestions.

8. Teachers should provide time, materials, and support for children to engage in mathematical play.
   This book includes center ideas and games that provide ample opportunities for play incorporating mathematical concepts.

9. Teachers should introduce mathematical concepts, activities, and vocabulary through a wide variety of experiences and teaching methods.
   This book helps teachers introduce math concepts through whole group experiences, small group experiences, individual activities, and free play.

10. Teachers should support children's learning through continual assessment of their mathematical knowledge and skills.
    This book provides suggestions for assessing students' skills through observations and through projects such as mini-books and hands-on activities.

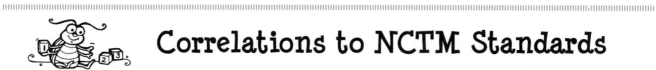

Correlations to NCTM Standards

This book supports the National Council for Teachers of Mathematics (NCTM) Principles and Standards for School Mathematics

The activities in this book support the following the following Number and Operations Standard Expectations for Grades Pre-K–2:

1. Students count and recognize the number of objects in a set.
   Many activities in this book support this standard.

2. Students understand the relative position and size of ordinal and cardinal numbers.
   Ordering and comparing activities in this book support this skill.

3. Students connect number words to numerals and to the quantities they represent using different physical representations.
   Many activities in this book require children to connect numerals to corresponding sets of quantities.

4. Students understand and represent common fractions such as $1/4$, $1/3$, and $1/2$.
   One activity in this book deals with dividing items in half.

The activities in this book support the following Algebra Standard Expectations for Grades Pre-K–2:

1. Students sort, classify, and order objects by a variety of properties.
   This book includes number ordering activities and object sorting activities.

2. Students recognize, describe, and extend simple sound, shape, or numeric patterns and change patterns from one form to another.
   Many activities in this book require children to recognize, describe, and extend object or shape patterns.

The activities in this book support the following Geometry Standard Expectations for Grades Pre-K–2:

1. Students identify, create, draw, compare, and sort two- and three-dimensional shapes.
   Many activities in this book have children identify, create, compare, and/or sort two-dimensional shapes.

2. Students describe characteristics and parts of two- and three-dimensional shapes.
   The Shape Stretch activity has children discuss the number of sides of geometric shapes.

3. Students can interpret the relative position of objects.
   Several activities in this book deal with the relative position of objects.

4. Students recognize geometric shapes in the world around them.
   The Shape Stretch activity has children find objects that correspond to certain geometric shapes.

The activities in this book support the following Measurement Standard Expectations for Grades Pre-K–2:

1. Students recognize the characteristics of length, volume, weight, area, and time.
   Activities in this book deal with length, volume, and weight measurements.

2. Students compare and order objects according to length, volume, weight, area, and/or time.
   This book includes length, volume, and weight comparison activities.

3. Students measure using standard and nonstandard units.
   In this book, children measure with nonstandard units.

4. Students measure with multiples of units of the same size, such as shoes, laid end to end.
   Several activities in this book have children measure length in this way.

5. Students use a variety of tools to measure.
   In this book, children learn to measure length, weight, and volume using a wide variety of tools.

6. Students develop the ability to make measurement comparisons and estimates.
   This book contains several measurement comparison and estimation activities.

The activities in this book support the following Data Analysis and Probability Standard Expectations for Grades Pre-K–2:

1. Students can sort and group objects according to their characteristics and organize information about the objects.
   Several activities in this book have children sort and group objects according to different characteristics.

2. Students can show data using objects, pictures, and graphs.
   One activity in this book has a suggestion for graphing data.